VIVEKANANDA
A Biography in Pictures

Arise, Awake, and Stop not till the Goal is Reached!

Advaita Ashrama
(Publication Department)
5 Dehi Entally Road • Kolkata 700 014

Published by
Swami Tattwavidananda
Adhyaksha, Advaita Ashrama
Mayavati, Champawat, Uttarakhand, Himalayas
from its Publication Department, Kolkata
Email: mail@advaitaashrama.org
Website: www.advaitaashrama.org

First Edition, November 1966
Seventh Edition, May 2007
Fourth Reprint, July 2014
3M3C

ISBN 978-81-7505-080-8

Printed in India at
Gipidi Box Co.
Kolkata 700 014

PREFACE TO THE SIXTH EDITION

In this edition several new photographs like those of (a) fourteen prominent monastic disciples of Swami Vivekananda (Chapter 9), (b) Raghumani Devi (Chapter 1), (c) Pramadadas Mitra (Chapter 3), (d) Pandit Shankar Pandurang (Chapter 3) and (e) Kate Sanborn (Chapter 4) have been added. Some photographs have been replaced by better ones while some others have been repositioned in the light of latest findings. It is hoped that these additions and changes will make the book more informative and attractive.

Kolkata
22 March 2005

PUBLISHER

PREFACE TO THE SECOND EDITION

THE first edition was not long in being sold out, and there has been a persistent demand for a second. We now have pleasure in offering a thoroughly-revised second edition. In the light of recent research, some pictures have been re-positioned. Two have been added to cover more adequately Swamiji's wanderings in Gujarat; and also two newly-discovered ones: (1) in a house-boat in Kashmir (p. 80), and (2) at Ridgely Manor (p. 87).

We trust this edition will be received with the same enthusiasm as the first.

Advaita Ashrama
Mayavati, Pithoragarh, Himalayas.
6 March 1973

PUBLISHER

PREFACE TO THE FIRST EDITION

DURING the birth centenary of Swami Vivekananda, which was observed recently in India and in many other parts of the world, need was keenly felt for a comprehensive album bringing together all the available pictures of Swami Vivekananda, as well as pictures concerning him. This album seeks to fulfil that need, and it is now presented as a humble offering to the memory of Swami Vivekananda whose life and teachings are a perennial source of inspiration and strength.

In his short but eventful life, Swami Vivekananda came in contact with many eminent people and visited many places in both East and West. Within the limitations of this album, it is not possible to include, though we wish we could, the pictures of all those persons and places. Every attempt has been made, however, to include as many as possible of the most important among them. It has been difficult to ascertain correctly the place and time of some pictures of the Swami. We have assigned these to the most probable place and time within the body of the book, but have added a note at the end, stating the other views regarding these pictures.

At the side of each picture is given either a quotation from the Swami's writings and spoken words or an account of a relevant incident in his life. By this means we have tried to provide an insight into his personality as well as an explanation of each picture.

The story of the Swami's life, as told through these pictures and their accompanying quotations or narrative, has been divided into seven chapters, and each chapter is introduced by an account of the Swami's life during that period. Thus the introductions to the chapters together constitute a connected but brief biography of the Swami. The eighth chapter is devoted to the Swami's brother-disciples, and includes photographs of them and the narration of some incident in their lives concerning Swami Vivekananda.

A list of acknowledgements is given below. In addition we extend our thanks to the many monks of the Ramakrishna Order and the many centres of the Ramakrishna Mission, and also to other friends, who have contributed photographs or blocks. Our thanks are also due to Swamis Gitananda and Smaranananda who have borne the brunt of the work, and to Mrs. Irene R. Ray, formerly of the Ramakrishna Mission Institute of Culture, Calcutta, who kindly went through the manuscript and the proofs.

Every effort has been made to make this album a worthy memorial to the Swami. It is our hope that through this new pictorial biography readers will be helped to a better understanding of the Swami and inspired to emulate the great ideals he preached and practised.

Mayavati
November, 1966

PUBLISHER

ACKNOWLEDGEMENTS

GRATEFUL acknowledgements are made to the following for lending the pictures indicated. (The number refers to the page, and the letter to the position of the picture on the page.)

To Swami Bhashyananda, Chicago, for 45 *a*, 55 *b*, 57 *a*, and 60 *a*; to Mrs. Marie Louise Burke, San Francisco, for 43 *a*, 46 *a* and *b*, 47 *a* and *b*, 48 *b*, 52 *a*, 55 *a*, and 57 *b* (all taken from her book, *Swami Vivekananda in America: New Discoveries*); to Harding Elizabeth Usha for 30 *c*; to Mellen, Gita, and Alvarado for 31 *a*; to the Consul-General of the Federal Republic of Germany, Calcutta, for 68 *a*; to the Embassy of the Federal Republic of Germany, New Delhi, for 68 *b*; to the Kashmir Sabha for 84 *a*; to Mohendra Publishing House, Calcutta, for 10 *a* and *b*, 11 *a* and *b*, 12 *a*, and 13 *a* and *b*; to Sri S. V. Nandagopal, Madurai, for 38 *a* and *b*, and 39 *b*; to the Ramakrishna Mission, Khetri, for 33 *a*; to the Ramakrishna Mission Home of Service, Varanasi, for 11 *b*, 32 *a*, and 100 *b*; to the Ramakrishna Mission Sarada Pitha, Belur (West Bengal) for 30 *b*; to the Ramakrishna Sarada Mission Sister Nivedita Girls' High School, Calcutta, for 67 *a*; to Swami Sarvajnananda, Nattarampalli, for 73 *b* and 74 *b*; to Swami Shambhavananda, Mysore, for 36 *b*; to Sri Beni Shankar Sharma, Calcutta, for 33 *b*; to Udbodhan Office, Calcutta, for 24 *b*, 65 *a*, 78 *a*, 90 *a*, 91 *b*, and 92 *a*; to the Centre Vedantique Ramakrishna, Paris, for 92 *b*; to the Vedanta Society of St. Louis for 10 *b*, 29 *b* and 113 *c*; to the Vedanta Society of Northern California, San Francisco, for 44 *a* and *b*, 45 *b*, 55 *b*, 56 *a*, 59 *a*, 61 *a*, 79 *a* and 103; to the Vedanta Society of Southern California, San Francisco, for 93 *a* and *b*, to the Vivekananda Rock Memorial Committee, Madras, for 37 *b*; to Ramakrishna Mission Institute of Culture, for 29 *a*; to Swami Atmasthananda, Sri Ramakrishna Ashrama, Rajkot, for 34 *a*; and to Swami Vivekananda's Ancestral House and Cultural Centre, for 11 *c*; to Ramakrishna Kutir, Almora, for 31 *b*; to Arka Naha, Calcutta, for 32 *a*.

CONTENTS

The Vision

I FOUND that my mind was soaring high in *samadhi* along a luminous path. It soon transcended the stellar universe and entered the subtler region of ideas.

As it ascended higher and higher, I found on both sides of the way ideal forms of gods and goddesses. The mind then reached the outer limits of that region, where a luminous barrier separated the sphere of relative existence from that of the Absolute. Crossing that barrier, the mind entered the transcendental realm, where no corporeal being was visible. Even the gods dared not peep into that sublime realm, and were content to keep their seats far below. But the next moment I saw seven venerable sages seated there in *samadhi.* It occurred to me that these sages must have surpassed not only men but even the gods in knowledge and holiness, in renunciation and love. Lost in admiration, I was reflecting on their greatness, when I saw a portion of that undifferentiated luminous region condense into the form of a divine child. The child came to one of the sages, tenderly clasped his neck with his lovely arms, and addressing him in a sweet voice, tried to drag his mind down from the state of *samadhi.* That magic touch roused the sage from the superconscious state, and he fixed his half-opened eyes upon the wonderful child. His beaming countenance showed that the child must have been the treasure of his heart. In great joy the strange child spoke to him, 'I am going down. You too must go with me.' The sage remained mute but his tender look expressed his assent. As he kept gazing at the child, he was again immersed in *samadhi.* I was surprised to find that a fragment of his body and mind was descending to earth in the form of a bright light. No sooner had I seen Narendra than I recognized him to be that sage.

— Sri Ramakrishna

(Quoted from *The Life of Swami Vivekananda* by His Eastern and Western Disciples, Vol. 1, p. 80-81)

Sri Ramakrishna
(1836–1886)

1

Early Days

SWAMI VIVEKANANDA or Narendranath Dutta, or simply Naren, as he was called in his pre-monastic days, was born to Vishwanath Dutta and Bhuvaneshwari Devi in Calcutta on Monday, 12 January 1863. The Dutta family was rich, respectable, and renowned for charity, learning, and a strong spirit of independence. Narendranath's grandfather, Durgacharan Dutta, was well-versed in Persian and Sanskrit and was skilled in law. But after the birth of his son Vishwanath, he renounced the world and became a monk. He was then only twenty-five years of age.

Vishwanath Dutta was an attorney-at-law in the Calcutta High Court. He was proficient in English and Persian, and took great delight in reciting to his family the poems of the Persian poet Hafiz. He also enjoyed the study of the Bible and of the Hindu scriptures in Sanskrit. Though charitable to an extravagant degree and sympathetic towards the poor, Vishwanath was rationalistic and progressive in outlook in matters religious and social, owing perhaps to the influence of Western culture. Bhuvaneshwari Devi was an accomplished lady with a regal bearing. She was deeply religious. Before the birth of Narendranath, though she had daughters, she yearned for a son and asked one of her relatives at Varanasi to make religious offerings to Vireshwara Shiva. It is said that she dreamt later that Lord Shiva promised to be born as her son. Narendranath was born some time afterwards. Among his brothers and sisters, his elder sister Swarnamayee Devi and his younger brothers Mahendranath Dutta and Bhupendranath Dutta survived him. Both the brothers were greatly accomplished and did not marry. Mahendranath led practically a monk's life, while Bhupendranath took a leading part in the revolutionary movement in Bengal in the early part of the twentieth century.

In his early childhood Narendranath was rather restless and given to much fun and frolic. But at the same time, he had a great attraction for spiritual matters and would play at worshipping or meditating on the images of Rama-Sita, Shiva, and others. The stories of the *Ramayana* and the *Mahabharata,* which his mother told him, left an indelible impression on his mind. Traits such as courage, sympathy for the poor, and attraction towards wandering monks appeared spontaneously in him. Even in childhood, Narendranath demanded convincing arguments for every proposition. With these qualities of head and heart, he grew into a vigorous youth.

Bhuvaneshwari Devi (1841–1911)

Referring to a lecture delivered by Swamiji at Boston on 'The Ideals of Indian Women', Mrs. Ole Bull wrote:

'Having given from the Vedas, from Sanskrit literature and the dramas these Ideals, and having cited the laws of today favourable to the women of India, he paid his filial homage to his own mother as having enabled him to do the best he had done, by her life of unselfish love and purity, that caused him by his very inheritance to choose the life of a monk.'

Raghumani Devi
(The maternal grandmother of Swami Vivekananda)

Bhuvaneshwari Devi, in her longing for a son, wrote to an old aunt of the Dutta family in Varanasi asking her to make the necessary offerings and prayers to Vireshwara Shiva that a son might be born to her.

Vireshwara Shiva

Vivekananda's ancestral house (foreground)
3 Gour Mohan Mukherjee Lane, Calcutta

The house of Vivekananda's Grandmother
7 Ramtanu Bose Lane, Calcutta

Narendra used to spend most of his time studying in an attic in his maternal grandmother's house at 9 Ramtanu Bose Lane. Sri Ramakrishna, grieved by Narendra's long absence from Dakshineshwar, went there one morning and met him on the staircase and asked in a faltering voice: 'Why don't you go there? Why don't you go there?' Then he gave him some sweets to eat and asked him to sing. Narendra sang: 'Awaken, O Mother Kundalini!'

Ancestral house before restoration

Vivekananda's ancestral house as it is today. It now houses a centre of the Ramakrishna Order.

Swarnamayee Devi, elder sister of Swami Vivekananda

Narendra was a naughty child, subject to fits of restlessness. What a tease he was! He would annoy his sisters and when chased would take refuge in the open drain, grinning and making faces at them in safety, for they would not follow him there.

In his boyhood Narendra used to tell his friends, 'I must become a *sannyasin*; a palmist predicted it,' and he would show them a certain straight line on his palm.

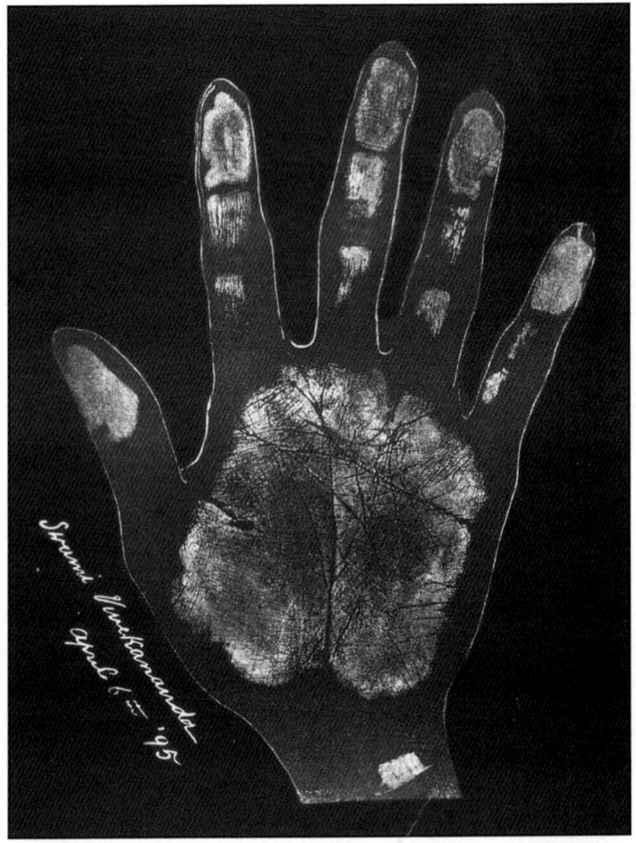

Swami Vivekananda's palm

Mahendranath Dutta (1869–1956)
Younger brother of Vivekananda

Bhupendranath Dutta (1880–1961)
Younger brother of Vivekananda

Both brothers together

'Kindly write Mohin that he has my blessings in whatever he does. ... I like boldness and adventure and my race stands in need of that spirit very much. ... Mohin must see his way to take care of mother and family. I am quite proud of him now.'

FROM A LETTER, 14 AUGUST 1900

2

At the Feet of Sri Ramakrishna

AS A YOUTH, Narendranath's leonine beauty was matched by his courage. He had the build of an athlete, a resonant voice, and a brilliant intellect. He distinguished himself in athletics and music, and among his colleagues was the undisputed leader.

Those who were Narendranath's friends and acquaintances at college remembered him as regal in his bearing, and self-confident, as though royally born. He attracted the attention of both Indian and English professors, who recognized his ambitious mind and the latent powers of his personality. About him Principal William Hastie said, 'Narendranath is really a genius. I have travelled far and wide but I have never yet come across a lad of his talents and possibilities, even in German universities, amongst philosophical students. He is bound to make his mark in life!'

Narendranath's college days were marked by tremendous intellectual ferment and spiritual upheaval. He was a lion among the students, defiant of conventional thought. He was vehement, of untiring energy, and his topics of conversation were endless. He now studied and absorbed Western thought, and this implanted a spirit of critical inquiry in his mind. His inborn tendency towards spirituality and his respect for ancient religious traditions and beliefs on the one side, and his rational mind coupled with his sharp intellect on the other, were now at war with each other. In this predicament he tried to find inspiration in the Brahmo Samaj, the popular socio-religious movement of the time. The Brahmo Samaj believed in a formless god, deprecated the worship of idols, and addressed itself to various forms of social reform. Narendranath also met prominent religious leaders, but could not get a convincing answer from them to his questions about the existence of God. This only increased his spiritual restlessness.

At this critical juncture, he remembered the words of his Professor, William Hastie, who had mentioned that a saint lived at Dakshineshwar, just outside Calcutta, who experienced the ecstasy described by Wordsworth in his poem, *The Excursion*. His cousin Ramchandra Dutta also induced him to visit the saint. Thus came about, in 1881, the historic meeting of these two great souls: the prophet of modern India and the bearer of his message. Narendranath asked: 'Sir, have you seen God?' Sri Ramakrishna answered his question in the affirmative: 'Yes, I have seen Him just as I see you here, only more intensely.' At last, here was one who could assure Narendranath from his own *experience* that God existed. His doubt was dispelled. The disciple's training had begun.

While Sri Ramakrishna tested him in many ways, Narendranath in turn also tested Sri Ramakrishna in order to ascertain the truth of his spiritual assertions. At one stage, after the passing away of his father in 1884, Narendranath's family suffered many troubles and privations. At the suggestion of his Master, Narendranath tried to pray to Mother Kali at Dakshineshwar for the alleviation of the family's distress. He found, however, that although his need was for wealth, he could pray only for knowledge and devotion.

Gradually, Narendranath surrendered himself to the Master. And Sri Ramakrishna, with infinite patience, calmed the rebellious spirit of his young disciple and led him forth from doubt to certainty and from anguish to spiritual bliss. But, more than Sri Ramakrishna's spiritual guidance and support, it was his love which conquered young Narendranath, love which the disciple reciprocated in full measure.

With Sri Ramakrishna's illness and his removal to Cossipore, on the outskirts of Calcutta, for treatment, began Narendranath's final training under his guru. It was a time remarkable for the intense spiritual fire which burned within him and which expressed itself through various intense practices. The Master utilized the opportunity to bring his young disciples under the leadership of Narendra. And when Narendra asked that he might be blessed with *nirvikalpa samadhi,* ordinarily regarded as the highest spiritual experience, the Master admonished him saying: 'Shame on you! I thought you would be like a huge banyan sheltering thousands from the scorching misery of the world. But now I see you seek your own liberation.' All the same, Narendra had the much-coveted realization, after which the Master said that the key to this would thenceforth remain in his keeping and the door would not be opened till Narendra had finished the task for which he had taken birth. Three or four days before his *mahasamadhi,* Sri Ramakrishna transmitted to Narendra his own power and told him: 'By the force of the power transmitted by me, great things will be done by you; only after that will you return to whence you came.'

The Master passed away in August 1886, and Narendranath and his other young disciples now passed through a very difficult period. Much later, in one of his lectures in America in 1900, Vivekananda was to say: 'Then came the sad day when our old teacher [Sri Ramakrishna] died.... We had no friends. Who would listen to a few boys, with their crank notions? Nobody. ... Why, everybody laughed. From laughter it became serious; it became persecution.... Who would sympathize with the imaginations of a boy—imaginations that caused so much suffering to others? ... None except one....' That one, as we shall see, was a woman—Sri Sarada Devi, the Holy Mother. She always stood behind her boys—her sons.

Many of the young disciples now gathered together in an old dilapidated house at Baranagore under the leadership of Narendra. Here, in the midst of a life of intense austerity and spiritual practices, the foundation of the Ramakrishna brotherhood was laid. It was during these days that Narendra, along with many of his brother-disciples, went to Antpur; and there on Christmas Eve (1886), sitting around a huge fire in the open, they took the vow of *sannyasa* (renunciation). The days at Baranagore were full of great joy, study, and spiritual practices. But the call of the wandering life of the *sannyasin* was now felt by most of the monks. And Narendra, too, towards the close of 1888, began to take temporary excursions away from the monastery.

General Assembly Institution (Scottish Church College)

Principal W. W. Hastie

In 1881 Narendra was studying in the General Assembly's Institution. One day, Professor W. W. Hastie, the Principal, was explaining Wordsworth's reference to trance in his poem *The Excursion*. 'Such an experience,' he said, 'is the result of purity of mind and concentration on some particular object, and it is rare indeed, particularly in these days. I have seen only one person who has experienced that blessed state of mind, and he is Ramakrishna Paramahamsa of Dakshineshwar. You can understand if you go there and see for yourself.'

The Dakshineshwar Temple (founded 1855): Sri Ramakrishna lived and taught here

Ramchandra, a relative of Narendra's father, had been brought up in their house, and was then a physician in Calcutta. When he came to know that Narendra declined to marry in order to pursue the path of spiritual enlightenment, he said to him, 'If you have a real desire to realize God, then come to the Master at Dakshineshwar instead of visiting the Brahmo Samaj and other places.'

Ramchandra Dutta

Narendra entered the room by the western door. He seemed careless about his body and dress, and, unlike other people, unmindful of the external world. His eyes bespoke an introspective mind, as if some part of it were always concentrated upon something within. I was surprised to find such a spiritual soul coming from the material atmosphere of Calcutta.

—Sri Ramakrishna

The western veranda of Sri Ramakrishna's room

Sri Ramakrishna's room at Dakshineshwar

Sri Ramakrishna in samadhi at a kirtan

'The thing is this: Sri Ramakrishna is far greater than his disciples understand him to be; **He** is the embodiment of infinite spiritual ideas capable of development in infinite ways. Even if one can find a limit to the knowledge of Brahman, one cannot measure the unfathomable depths of our Master's mind! One gracious glance of his eyes can create a hundred thousand Vivekanandas at this instant! If he chooses now instead to work through me, making me his instrument, I can only bow to his will.'

Mother Bhavatarini at Dakshineshwar

In the beginning of his discipleship, Narendra denounced image-worship. But, after his father's sudden death, when he had to witness the heart-rending sight of extreme poverty at home, he was forced to approach Sri Ramakrishna and request him to plead with Mother Kali (Mother Bhavatarini) on his behalf. The Master, however, sent Narendra to pray personally, who later described his experience thus:

'Reaching the temple, as I cast my eyes on the image, I actually found that the Divine Mother was living and conscious, the perennial fountain of divine love and beauty. I was caught in a surging wave of devotion and love. In an ecstasy of joy, I prostrated myself again and again before the Mother and prayed, "Mother, give me discrimination! Give me renunciation! Give unto me knowledge and devotion! Grant that I may have an uninterrupted vision of Thee!" A serene peace reigned in my soul. The world was forgotten. Only the Divine Mother shone within my heart.'

The Panchavati at Dakshineshwar where Sri Ramakrishna and, later, his disciples practised many spiritual disciplines.

'After all, I am only the boy who used to listen with wrapt wonderment to the wonderful words of Sri Ramakrishna under the banyan at Dakshineshwar. That is my true nature; works and activities, doing good and so forth are all superimpositions.'

FROM A LETTER, 18 APRIL 1900

In Calcutta, 1886

One day, at Cossipore, Narendra was meditating under a tree with Girish Ghosh, another disciple of Sri Ramakrishna. The place was infested with mosquitoes. Girish tried in vain to concentrate his mind. Casting his eyes on Naren, he saw him absorbed in meditation, though his body was covered by a blanket of mosquitoes.

'Behold! Here is Naren. See! See! Oh, what power of insight he has! It is like the shoreless sea of radiance! The Mother, Mahamaya Herself, cannot approach within less than ten feet of him! She is barred by the very glory which She has imparted to him!'

—Sri Ramakrishna

At Cossipore Garden, 1886

Cossipore Garden House

'It will be good if we can get the garden of Kristo Gopal at Cossipore. ... All our associations centre round that garden. In reality that is our first Math. ... Make special efforts for Cossipore.'

—From a letter, 13 July 1897

To Naren, standing by the Master's bedside, a couple of days before his *mahasamadhi*, came the thought: 'If he can say now, when he is in the throes of death, "I am God incarnate", then I will believe him.' The Master at once turned towards him and said: 'O my Naren, are you still not convinced? He who was Rama and Krishna is now Ramakrishna in this body—but not from the standpoint of your Vedanta.'

Sri Ramakrishna's room at Cossipore

After Sri Ramakrishna's passing away, 16 August 1886

(1) Mahendra or M. (3) Kali (5) Sarat (6) Mani Mallick (7) Gangadhar (8) Navagopal (9) Surendra Mitra (11) Tarak (13) the elder Gopal (15) Vaikuntha (17) Manmohan (18) Harish (19) Narayan (21) Sashi (22) Latu (23) Bhavanath (24) Baburam (25) Niranjan (26) Narendra (27) Ramchandra Dutta (28) Balaram Bose (29) Rakhal (30) Nityagopal (31) Yogindra (32) Devendranath Mazumdar

Surendranath Mitra (1850–1890)

After the passing away of the Master, some of the young men, headed by Narendra, were determined not to go back to their homes. But how and where were they to live? At this time, Surendranath Mitra, the lay devotee who had borne the major part of the expenses of the Master's treatment at Cossipore, had a strange vision. One evening, Sri Ramakrishna appeared to him in a vision and asked him to aid the boys who were in such a sad plight. He went at once to them and said: 'Brothers, where will you go? Let me rent a house where you may stay together, and where we householders may find a temporary refuge from the worries of the world.'

The building was a dreary, deserted place, very old and sadly in need of repairs. It was also said to be haunted. Indeed, nobody else would have lived there. This house was rented at Rs. 10 a month and became the Baranagaore monastery.

The Baranagore Math

Group at Baranagore Math in 1887

Standing (left to right): Swami Shivananda, Swami Ramakrishnananda, Swami Vivekananda, the monastery cook, Deven Majumdar, Mahendranath Gupta (M.), Swami Trigunatitananda, Mustaphi (maternal uncle of Deven Majumdar)
Sitting (left to right): Swami Niranjanananda, Swami Saradananda, Hootka Gopal, and Swami Abhedananda

'There were days at the Baranagore Math when we had nothing to eat. Boiled leaves of the bimba creeper, salt, and rice—this was our diet for months! Come what would, we were indifferent. We were being carried on in a strong tide of religious practices and meditation.'

After the passing away of the Master, the monks at the Baranagore Math depended on Balaram for many things. When ill or on duty in Calcutta, they found a ready welcome at Balaram's house. In the early days of the Baranagore monastery, Balaram once went there to find that the young monks had nothing to eat except rice and some cooked greens. Returning home he told his wife that he would eat those two things only that day. After this Balaram liberally supplied the monks with all the necessary articles of food.

Balaram Bose (1842-1890)

Antpur, where the sacred fire was lighted (where the stone slab stands now).

Mahendranath Gupta (1854–1932) the author of 'The Gospel of Sri Ramakrishna'

From Antpur, Swamiji wrote to him on 7 February 1889, when he received the manuscript of *Sri Ramakrishna Kathamrita (The Gospel of Sri Ramakrishna)*:

'I thank you a hundred times, Master! You have hit Ramakrishna on the right point.

Few, alas, understand him!

'My heart leaps with joy—and it is a wonder that I do not go mad when I find anybody thoroughly launched into the midst of the doctrine which is to shower peace on earth hereafter.'

3

The Wandering Monk

A REMARKABLE change of outlook came over Narendra between the closing of 1888, when he first left on his temporary excursions, and 1890, when he parted from his brethren and travelled alone as an unknown mendicant. He began to assume various names in order to conceal his identity that he might be swallowed up in the immensity of India.

Now it was that the natural desire of an Indian monk for a life of solitude gave way to the prescience that he was to fulfil a great destiny; that his was not the life of an ordinary recluse struggling for personal salvation. Under the influence of his burning desire to know India better and the mute appeal rising all around him from oppressed India, he went first to Varanasi, the holiest city of the Hindus. There he met Pramadadas Mitra, a great Sanskrit scholar, with whom he had been in correspondence regarding various problems of Hindu religion and philosophy.

After Varanasi he visited Lucknow, Agra, Vrindavan, Hathras, and Hrishikesh, and then returned to Baranagore for a time. At Hathras, he met Sharatchandra Gupta who became his first disciple (Swami Sadananda). He revealed to him the mission entrusted to him by his Master, namely, the spiritual regeneration of India and the world. Sharat, who was on the staff of the railway station at Hathras, resigned his post and followed his guru to help him in his mission.

An important event in the Swami's life occurred at this time when in 1890 he met Pavhari Baba of Ghazipur, for whose saintliness he had great admiration throughout his life. At this time, he was torn between the desire, on the one hand, to become absorbed in the eternal silence of the Absolute and, on the other, to fulfil his Master's mission. He hoped that Pavhari Baba would fulfil his intense longing for the highest absorption in the Divine, and even thought of becoming his disciple for this purpose. For twenty-one days Narendra was on the point of yielding to this temptation, but repeated visions of Sri Ramakrishna and Pavhari Baba's unwillingness to teach drew him away from this resolve.

In July 1890, the Swami took leave of Sri Sarada Devi, the holy consort of Sri Ramakrishna, who was the spiritual guide of the young monks after the Master's death. He also took leave of his brother monks, with the firm resolve to cut himself free from all ties and to go into the solitude of the Himalayas, for he felt it essential to be alone. In the words of Romain Rolland: 'This was the great departure. Like a diver he plunged into the Ocean of India and the Ocean of India covered his tracks. Among its flotsam and jetsam he was nothing more than one nameless sannyasin in saffron robe among a thousand others. But the fires of genius burned in his eyes. He was a prince despite all disguise.'

His wanderings took him to various places of pilgrimage and historical interest in Uttar Pradesh, Rajasthan, Gujarat, Maharashtra, Tamil Nadu, Karnataka, Hyderabad, and Kerala. Everywhere the glory of ancient India vividly came before his eyes, whether political, cultural, or spiritual. In the midst of this great education, the abject misery of the Indian masses stood out before his mind. He moved from one princely State to another, everywhere to explore avenues of mitigating their lot. Thus he came to meet many leading personalities and rulers of the princely States. Among them, Maharaja Ajit Singh of Khetri became his fast friend and ardent disciple. At Alwar he studied the *Mahabhashya* of Patanjali. At Poona, the Swami met Bal Gangadhar Tilak, the great national leader. At first Tilak talked with the Swami with scant regard, but later, impressed by the Swami's depth of learning and profundity of thought, he invited him to be his guest. From there, after a stay at Belgaum, he went to Bangalore and Mysore. The Maharaja of Mysore gave him the assurance of financial support to enable him to go to the West to seek help for India and to preach the eternal religion. From Mysore, he visited Trivandrum and Kanyakumari.

But wherever he went it was not the important places and people that drew his attention. It was the terrible poverty and misery of the masses that caused his soul to burn in agony. He had travelled through the whole of India, often on foot, for nearly three years, coming to know India at first hand. Now he had reached the end of his journey as it were. He prostrated himself with great feeling before the image of Mother Kumari at the Kanyakumari temple. Then he swam across the sea to a rock off the south coast, and sitting there he went into deep meditation. The vast panorama of his experiences during his travels passed before his mind's eye. He meditated on the past, the present, and the future of India, the causes of her downfall, and the means of her resurrection. He then took the momentous decision to go to the West to seek help for the poor of India and thus give shape to his life's mission.

With this decision, he journeyed to Rameshwaram and Madurai. At the latter place, he met the Raja of Ramnad who became his staunch supporter and assured him of his help. He then went on to Madras, where a group of young men, headed by Alasinga Perumal, were eagerly awaiting his arrival. To them he revealed his intention of visiting America to attend the Parliament of Religions that was being convened at Chicago. His young disciples forthwith raised a subscription for his passage. But the Swami was not yet certain that it was the Divine Mother's will that he should go, and so he asked them to give away the money to the poor. At this juncture, the Swami had a symbolic dream in which Sri Ramakrishna walked out into the sea and beckoned him to follow. This, coupled with the blessings and permission of Sri Sarada Devi, who also, in a dream, had received Sri Ramakrishna's consent, settled the question for him, and his young friends again set about collecting the necessary funds.

He next paid a short visit to Hyderabad. Then, while arrangements were being made for his journey to America, there came a sudden invitation from the Maharaja of Khetri to attend the celebrations in connection with the birth of his son. The Swami could not refuse this invitation from his disciple. The Maharaja received him cordially and promised to help him in every possible way. True to his word, the Maharaja sent his personal secretary with the Swami to equip him for the journey and see him off at Bombay. His journey to America commenced on 31 May 1893.

Vivekananda as a Wandering Monk

Have thou no home. What home can hold thee friend?
The sky thy roof, the grass thy bed; and food
What chance may bring, well cooked or ill, judge not.
No food or drink can taint that noble Self
Which knows Itself. Like rolling river free
Thou ever be, Sannyasin bold! say—'Om Tat Sat Om'

From *The Song of the Sannyasin*

Varanasi: View of a ghat

One day, as Swamiji was returning from the temple of Mother Durga, he was pursued by a troop of monkeys. Fearing that they might harm him, he began to run. Suddenly, he heard the voice of an old *sannyasin* calling out to him: 'Stop! Always face the brutes!' Swamiji turned; his fear gone. Seeing him defiant, the monkeys fled. Years later, in a lecture given in New York, he referred to this incident and pointed out the moral of the story: 'So face nature! Face ignorance! Face illusion! Never fly!'

The Durga Temple at Varanasi

Pramadadas Mitra

Pramadadas Mitra's house at Varanasi

When taking leave of Pramada Babu some time in 1890, Swamiji said: 'When I shall return here next time, I shall burst upon society like a bomb-shell, and it will follow me like a dog.' And he did not return to this sacred city until he had verily stirred up the world to new modes of thought and resurrected the spirit of the Indian sages.

Swamiji remembered the life of freedom of the stern ascetics in the neighbourhood of Hardwar and Hrishikesh. 'I saw many great men in Hrishikesh,' said the Swami in later life. 'One case that I remember was that of a man who seemed to be mad. He was coming nude down the street, with boys pursuing and throwing stones at him. The man was bubbling over with laughter, while blood was streaming down his face and neck. I took him and bathed his wound, putting ashes (made by burning a piece of cloth) on it to stop the bleeding. And all the time, with peals of laughter, he told me of the fun the boys and he had been having, throwing the stones. "So the Father plays", he said.'

Hardwar

Peepul tree at Kakrighat, on the way to Almora

Lala Badri Sah's House, where Swamiji stayed at Almora

Swamiji left Baranagore Math with Swami Akhandananda in July 1890 for performing spiritual austerities in the Himalayas. Describing to the latter an experience he had at Kakrighat on his way to Almora, he said pointing to a peepul tree, 'Under this tree one of the greatest problems of my life was solved.' Then he told of his wonderful vision about the oneness of the microcosm and the macrocosm.

While at Almora, Swamiji was the guest of Lala Badri Sah. The Swami was much impressed with Badri Sah's devotion and hospitality and remarked that he had rarely seen a devotee like him.

Nakki Lake, Mt. Abu

In the summer of 1891, Swamiji visited Mt. Abu in Rajasthan and stayed in a cave on the banks of the Nakki Lake. Later, at the importunate request of a Muslim pleader, he went to stay in his house. After a few days, the pleader invited Munshi Jagmohanlal, the private secretary of the Maharaja of Khetri, to meet the Swami. Jagmohanlal asked Swamiji: 'Well, Swamiji, you are a Hindu monk. How is it that you are living with a Muslim? Your food may now and then be touched by him.' At this question Swamiji flared up. He said: 'Sir, what do you mean? I am a *sannyasin*. I am above all social conventions. I can dine even with a *bhangi* (sweeper). ... I see Brahman everywhere, manifested even in the meanest creature. For me there is nothing high or low. Shiva, Shiva!'

Dilwara Temple

While at Mount Abu, Swamiji spent many days examining the glories of the Dilwara Temple, which is said to be one of the most wonderful temples in India. For the delicacy and beauty of its sculpture it is almost unrivalled in the land. It was built in the early part of the thirteenth century by two pious brothers, merchant princes, and is said to have taken fourteen years to build.

The Swami passed many weeks with the Maharaja of Khetri, studying, teaching, and living the spiritual life. Though in a palace, he lived as a monk, in constant communion with his soul and his Master. Swamiji often visited the houses of his poorer devotees, and frequently ate at the house of Pundit Shankar Lal, a poor Brahmin. The whole town of Khetri was enamoured of the Swami, and he treated the least of his admirers with the same love and affection as he showed to the Maharaja.

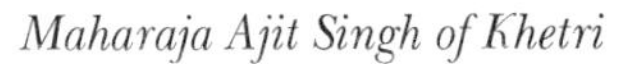

Maharaja Ajit Singh of Khetri

The palace of the Maharaja of Khetri where Vivekananda stayed. It now houses a centre of the Ramakrishna Order.

On his arrival at Junagadh, the Swami was keen to climb up the Girnar mountain, sacred to Buddhism and Jainism, and also to many creeds of Hinduism. He climbed up with ease the steep mountain path and arrived first at the large enclosure of sixteen Jaina temples. He paused here to study their marvellous architecture and, proceeding further, he reached the summit. From there he saw the whole of India, as it were, as a place of pilgrimage, as one huge temple filled with shrines and sanctuaries.

Jaina temples on Mt. Girnar

The house of Pundit Shankar Pandurang, where Swamiji stayed while in Porbandar. It now houses a centre of the Ramakrishna Order.

Pundit Shankar Pandurang

The Swami's stay at Porbandar on the Saurashtra coast was unusually long. The Maharaja insisting, he remained here for eleven months and worked with Pundit Shankar Pandurang, a Vedic scholar of repute, in translating the Vedas. Here he also finished his study of the *Mahabhashya,* Patanjali's great commentary on Panini's grammar. He also took up the study of French and gained a fair knowledge of it with the help of the Pundit who said, 'It will be of use to you, Swamiji.'

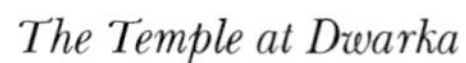

The Temple at Dwarka

Swamiji came as a wandering monk to Dwaraka, holy with innumerable memories and legends of Sri Krishna. But of its glories nothing remains at the present day. Now the tumultuous ocean roars over the place where once stood the great capital of which Sri Krishna was the reigning prince. Gazing out upon the ocean, waves of agony rose in the Swami's mind at the thought that nothing remained but the ruins of that Greater India. He sat on the shore and yearned ardently to fathom the India of the future. Later, in the silence of his room, he saw a great light, symbolizing the bright future of India.

When the Parliament was in session, the organizers lodged Swamiji in the house of Mr. and Mrs. John B. Lyon. He reached there after midnight and Mrs. Lyon received him cordially, though she was not sure how her guests, some of whom were Southerners and did not like coloured people, would react to the situation.

Mrs. John B. Lyon

Mr. John B. Lyon

Next morning, about half an hour before breakfast, Mr. Lyon went in the library to read the morning papers. There he found the Swami, and, before breakfast was served, he went to his wife and said: 'I don't care a bit, Emily, if all our guests leave! The Indian is the most brilliant and interesting man who has ever been in our house and he shall stay as long as he wishes.'

In Chicago, 1893

The going forth of Vivekananda, marked out by the Master as the heroic soul destined to take the world between his two hands and change it, was the first visible sign to the world that India was awake, not only to survive but to conquer.

Sri Aurobindo

The Parliament of Religions opened on the morning of 11 September 1893 at the Art Insitute in Chicago. It was in the Institute's great Hall of Columbus that the delegates of the Parliament gathered on that memorable morning. At ten o'clock, ten solemn strokes of the New Liberty Bell, on which was inscribed, 'A new commandment I give unto you, that ye love one another', proclaimed the opening of the Congress—each stroke representing one of the ten chief religions.

The Art Institute of Chicago

The Parliament of Religions in Chicago, 27 September 1893

'Men from all nations were there. ... There was a grand procession, and we were all marshalled on to the platform. Imagine a hall below and a huge gallery above, packed with six or seven thousand men and women representing the best culture of the country, and on the platform learned men of all the nations of the earth. ... They were all prepared and came with ready-made speeches. I was a fool and had none, but bowed down to Devi Sarasvati and stepped up, and Dr. Barrows introduced me. I made a short speech, ... and when it was finished, I sat down almost exhausted.'

From a letter to Alasinga,
2 November 1893

At the Parliament of Religions

At the Parliament of Religions

At the Parliament of Religions

'"Children of immortal bliss"—what a sweet, what a hopeful name! Allow me to call you, brethren, by that sweet name—heirs of immortal bliss—yea, the Hindu refuses to call you sinners. Ye are the children of God, the sharers of immortal bliss, holy and perfect beings. Ye divinities on earth—sinners! It is a sin to call a man so; it is a standing libel on human nature. Come up, O lions, and shake off the delusion that you are sheep; you are souls immortal, spirits free, blest and eternal.'

'Sectarianism, bigotry, and its horrible descendant, fanaticism, have long possessed this beautiful earth. They have filled the earth with violence, drenched it often with human blood, destroyed civilization and sent whole nations to despair. Had it not been for these horrible demons, human society would be far more advanced than it is now.'

Vivekananda as a Delegate to the Parliament of Religions

At the Parliament of Religions

'If anybody dreams of the exclusive survival of his own religion and the destruction of the others, I pity him from the bottom of my heart, and point out to him that upon the banner of every religion will soon be written in spite of resistance: "Help and not Fight", "Assimilation and not Destruction", and "Harmony and Peace and not Dissension".'

'By far the most important and typical representative of Hinduism was Swami Vivekananda, who, in fact, was beyond question the most popular and influential man in the Parliament, ... and on all occasions he was received with greater enthusiasm than any other speaker—Christian or Pagan. The people thronged about him wherever he went and hung with eagerness on his every word. The most rigid of orthodox Christians say of him, "He is indeed a prince among men."'

MERWIN-MARIE SNELL
President of the scientific section
of the Parliament of Religions

On the platform at the Parliament of Religions

Swami Vivekananda and Narasimhacharya, Chicago, 1893

'Shall India die? Then from the world all spirituality will be extinct, all moral perfection will be extinct, all sweet-souled sympathy for religion will be extinct, all ideality will be extinct; and in its place will reign the duality of lust and luxury as the male and female deities; with money as its priest, fraud, force, and competition its ceremonies, and the human soul its sacrifice. Such a thing can never be.'

FROM A LETTER TO THE HINDUS OF MADRAS, SEPTEMBER 1894

Indian Group at Chicago, 11 September, 1893

Left to right : Narasimhacharya, Lakshminarayan, Swami Vivekananda, Dharmapala, and Virchand Gandhi

In Chicago, September 1893

'I was at the Parliament of Religions in Chicago in 1893. When that young man got up and said "Sisters and Brothers of America", seven thousand people rose to their feet as a tribute to something they knew not what. When it was over, I saw scores of women walking over the benches to get near him, and I said to myself, "Well, my lad, if you can resist that onslaught, you are indeed a God!"'

MRS. S. K. BLODGETT
in her reminiscences

In Chicago, September 1893

At the Parliament of Religions

In Chicago, 1893

'Man is to become divine by realizing the divine. Idols or temples or churches or books are only the supports, the helps of his spiritual childhood: but on and on he must progress.'

In Chicago, October 1893

'Each soul is potentially divine. The goal is to manifest this Divinity within, by controlling nature, external and internal. Do this either by work, or worship, or psychic control, or philosophy—by one or more or all of these—and be free. This is the whole of religion. Doctrines, or dogmas, or rituals, or books, or temples, or forms, are but secondary details.'

'The other night the camp people went to sleep beneath a pine tree under which I sit every morning *à la* Hindu and talk to them. Of course, I went with them, and we had a nice night under the stars, sleeping on the lap of mother earth, and I enjoyed every bit of it. I cannot describe to you that night's glories—after a year of brutal life that I have led, to sleep on the ground, to meditate under the tree in the forest !'

FROM A LETTER FROM GREENACRE,
31 JULY 1894

At Greeanacre, August 1894 (both pictures)

At Greenacre, August 1894

'A while back several hundred intellectual men and women were gathered in a place called Greenacre, and I was there for nearly two months. Every day I would sit in our Hindu fashion under a tree, and my followers and disciples would sit on the grass all around me. Every morning I would instruct them, and how earnest they were.'

FROM A LETTER, SEPTEMBER 1894

In New York, 1895

'Dream no more! Oh, dream no more, my soul! In one word, I have a message to give, I have no time to be sweet to the world, and every attempt at sweetness makes me a hypocrite. I will die a thousand deaths rather than lead a jellyfish existence and yield to every requirement of this foolish world, no matter whether it be my own country or a foreign country. You are mistaken, utterly mistaken, if you think I have a *work*, as Mrs. Bull thinks; I have *no work* under or beyond the sun. I have a message, and I will give it after my own fashion. I will neither Hinduise my message, nor Christianise it, nor make it any "ise" in the world. I will only my-ise it, and that is all. *Liberty*, Mukti, is all my religion, and everything that tries to curb it, I will avoid by fight or flight.'

Robert Ingersoll, agnostic philosopher and orator

'Ingersoll once said to me', said the Swami in the course of a class talk, 'I believe in making the most of this world, in squeezing the orange dry, because this world is all we are sure of.' I replied: 'I know a better way to squeeze the orange of this world than you do; and I get more out of it. I *know* I cannot die, so I am not in a hurry. I know that there is no fear, so I enjoy the squeezing. I have no duty, no bondage of wife and children and property; and so I can love all men and women. Everyone is God to me. Think of the joy of loving man as God! Squeeze your orange this way and get ten thousandfold more out of it. Get every single drop.'

Mme Emma Calve

Madame Emma Calve, the famous opera singer, who had the greatest admiration for Swamiji, wrote about him: 'It has been my good fortune and my joy to know a man who truly "walked with God", a noble being, a saint, a philosopher, and a true friend. His influence upon my spiritual life was profound. He opened up new horizons before me, enlarging and unifying my religious ideas and ideals; teaching me a broader understanding of truth. My soul will bear him eternal gratitude.'

Mrs. Mary C. Funke wrote of her delightful experience at the Thousand Island Park: 'There were twelve of us and it seemed as if Pentecostal fire descended and touched the Master. One afternoon, when he had been telling us of the glory of renunciation, of the joy and freedom of those of the ochre robe, he suddenly left us, and in a short time he had written his 'Song of the Sannyasin', a very passion of sacrifice and renunciation. I think the thing which impressed me most in those days was his infinite patience and gentleness—as of a father with his children, though most of us were several years older than he.'

At Thousand Island Park

Miss Dutcher's cottage at Thousand Island Park

At Thousand Island Park on the river St. Lawrence, Swamiji lived in Miss Dutcher's cottage from June 1895 for seven weeks, teaching intimately a group of twelve disciples. The upper open window in the left-hand wing of the house belonged to the Swami's room. The Swami's piazza was where the evening talks were given and the Swami's seat was at the end near his room. The house is now used as a retreat by the Ramakrishna-Vivekananda Centre, New York.

Mrs. John J. Bagley

Mrs. Bagley wrote in a letter about him: 'Every human being would be made better by knowing him and living in the same house with him. ... I want everyone in America to know Vivekananda, and if India has more such let her send them to us.'

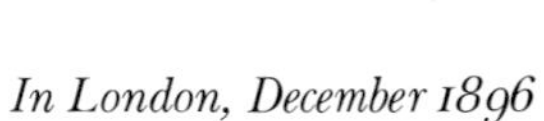

In London, December 1896

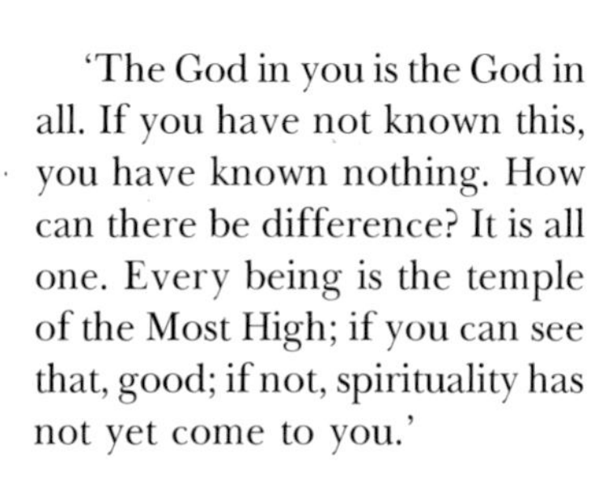

'The God in you is the God in all. If you have not known this, you have known nothing. How can there be difference? It is all one. Every being is the temple of the Most High; if you can see that, good; if not, spirituality has not yet come to you.'

'It is good and very grand to conquer external nature, but grander still to conquer our internal nature. It is grand and good to know the laws that govern the stars and planets; it is infinitely grander and better to know the laws that govern the passions, the feelings, the will of mankind. This conquering of the inner man, understanding the secrets, belong entirely to religion.'

In London, May 1896
(both pictures)

'The religious ideals of the future must embrace all that exists in the world and is good and great, and at the same time, have infinite scope for future development. All that was good in the past must be preserved; and the doors must be kept open for future additions to the already existing store.'

'Men are taught from childhood that they are weak and sinners. Teach them that they are all glorious children of immortality, even those who are the weakest in manifestation. Let positive, strong, helpful thoughts enter into their brains from the very childhood. Lay yourselves open to these thoughts, and not to weakening and paralysing ones.'

In London, December 1896 (both pictures)

'The old religion said that he was an atheist who did not believe in God. The new religion says that he is an atheist who does not believe in himself.'

In London, July 1896

'Another peculiarity of the Advaitic system is that from its very start it is non-destructive. This is another glory, the boldness to preach, "Do not disturb the faith of any, even of those who through ignorance have attached themselves to lower forms of worship." This philosophy preaches a God who is the sum total. If you seek a universal religion which can apply to everyone, that religion must not be composed of only the parts, but it must always be their sum total and include all degrees of religious development.

In London, December 1896

'So work, says Vedanta, putting God in everything, and knowing Him to be in everything. Work incessantly, holding life as something deified, as God Himself, and knowing that this is all we have to do, this is all we should ask for. God is in everything, where else shall we go to find Him? He is already in every work, every thought, in every feeling. Thus knowing, we must work—this is the only way, there is no other.'

In London, December 1896

'You know, of course, the steadiness of the English; they are the least jealous of each other of all nations, and that is why they dominate the world. They have solved the secret of obedience without slavish cringing—great freedom with great law-abidingness.'

FROM A LETTER, 8 OCTOBER 1896

In London, 1896

On the eve of his departure an English friend asked Swamiji: 'Swami, how do you like your motherland now after four years' experience of the luxurious, glorious, powerful West?' His significant reply was: 'India I loved before I came away. Now the very dust of India has become holy to me, the very air is now to me holy, it is now the holy land, the place of pilgrimage, the *tirtha*!'

Sister Nivedita

'Let me tell you frankly that I am now convinced that you have a great future in the work of India. What was wanted was not a man, but a woman; a real lioness, to work for the Indians, women specially.

'India cannot yet produce great women, she must borrow them from other nations. Your education, sincerity, purity, immense love, determination, and above all, the Celtic blood make you just the woman wanted.'

FROM A LETTER TO NIVEDITA,
29 JULY 1897

J. J. Goodwin

At the news of Goodwin's premature death, Swamiji wrote: 'The debt of gratitude I owe him can never be repaid, and those who think they have been helped by any thought of mine, ought to know that almost every word of it was published through the untiring and most unselfish exertions of Mr. Goodwin. In him I have lost a friend true as steel, a disciple of never-failing devotion, a worker who knew not what tiring was, and the world is less rich by one of those few who are born, as it were, to live only for others.'

Professor Max Müller

'I had a beautiful visit with Professor Max Müller. He is a saint—a Vedantist through and through. ... He has been a devoted admirer of my old Master for years.

FROM A LETTER, 30 MAY 1896

'What an extraordinary man is Professor Max Müller! I paid a visit to him a few days ago. I should say, that I went to pay my respects to him, for whosoever loves Sri Ramakrishna, whatever be his or her sect, or creed, or nationality, my visit to that person I hold as a pilgrimage. ... "Ramakrishna is worshipped today by thousands, Professor," I said. "To whom else shall worship be accorded, if not to such?" was the answer.'

Professor Paul Deussen

Swamiji was invited by Professor Paul Deussen to his residence in Kiel. Some time during the day, the Professor found the Swami turning over the pages of a poetical work. He spoke to him, but got no response. When the Swami came to know of it later, he apologized, saying that he was so absorbed in reading that he had not heard him. The Professor was not satisfied with this explanation until, in the course of conversation, the Swami quoted and interpreted verses from the book. Dr. Deussen was dumbfounded and asked the Swami how he could accomplish such a feat of memory.

'I am much refreshed now. I look out of the window and see the huge glaciers just before me and feel that I am in the Himalayas. I am quite calm. My nerves have regained their accustomed strength; and little vexations, like those you write of, do not touch me at all. How shall I be disturbed by this child's play? The whole world is a mere child's play—preaching, teaching, and all included.'

FROM A LETTER, 8 AUGUST 1896

Saas-Fee, Switzerland, which Swamiji visited on 8 August 1896

While Swamiji was in Switzerland, he said: 'O, I long for such a monastery where I can retire from the labours of my life and pass the rest of my days in meditation. It will be a centre for work and meditation, where my Indian and Western disciples can live together, and them I shall train as workers, the former to go out as preachers of Vedanta to the West, and the latter to devote their lives to the good of India.' Capt. Sevier said: 'How nice it would be, Swamiji, if this could be done. We must have such a monastery.' And it was in 1899 that Capt. and Mrs. Sevier established the Advaita Ashrama at Mayavati in the Himalayas.

'I remembered in England Capt. and Mrs. Sevier, who have clad me when I was cold, nursed me better than my own mother would have, borne with me in my weaknesses, my trials: and they have nothing but blessings for me. And that Mrs. Sevier, because she did not care for honour, has the worship of thousands today: and when she is dead, millions will remember her as one of the great benefactresses of the poor Indians.'

FROM A LETTER, NOVEMBER 1899

Mrs. J. H. Sevier

Capt. J. H. Sevier

5

Triumphal Return

SWAMI VIVEKANANDA left London with the Seviers on 16 December, and after a visit to Rome and other places in Italy, he took the boat for India at Naples on 30 December. At Naples, Mr. Goodwin joined the party. They reached Colombo on 15 January 1897. The news of the Swami's return had already reached India and the people everywhere, throughout the country, were afire with enthusiasm to receive him. He was no more the unknown *sannyasin.* In every city, small or big, committees had been formed to give him a fitting reception. Eye-witness accounts give a glowing picture of the reception accorded to the Swami at Colombo. The crowd that had assembled saw the launch carrying the Swami steaming towards the jetty, and their din and clamour of shouts and hand-clapping drowned even the noise of the breaking waves. A grand reception was given to him in a city hall. The Swami, who had decided to sail straight to Madras, was forced to change his plans and proceed by the overland route, in view of the enthusiasm of the people in Ceylon and Southern India. As Romain Rolland says, the Swami 'replied to the frenzied expectancy of the people by his Message to India, a conch sounding the resurrection of the land of Rama, of Shiva, of Krishna, and calling the heroic Spirit, the immortal Atman, to march to war. He was a general, explaining his *Plan of Campaign,* and calling his people to rise *en masse*: "My India, arise! Where is your vital force? In your Immortal Soul."' At Madras he delivered five public lectures, every one of which was a clarion call to throw away weakness and superstition and rise to build a new India. He emphasized that in India 'the keynote of the whole music of the national life' was religion, a religion which preached the 'spiritual oneness of the whole universe and when that was strengthened everything else would take care of itself. He did not spare his criticism, however, castigating his countrymen for aping the West, for their blind adherence to old superstitions, for their caste prejudices, and so on.

From Madras the Swami travelled to Calcutta and arrived there on 20 February. His native city gave him a grand welcome, and here the Swami paid a touching tribute to his Master: 'If there has been anything achieved by me, by thoughts, or words, or deeds, if from my lips has ever fallen one word that has helped anyone in the world, I lay no claim to it, it was his. ... If this nation wants to rise, take my word for it, it will have to rally round his name.'

To establish his work on a firm basis, the Swami summoned all the monastic and lay disciples to a meeting at Balaram Bose's house, and the Ramakrishna Mission was formed on 1 May 1897. The aims and ideals of the Mission propounded by the Swami were purely spiritual and humanitarian. He had inaugurated the machinery for carrying out his ideas.

It may be mentioned that the plan of work propounded by Swamiji was not accepted without some opposition. However, Holy Mother, knowing him to be the Master's instrument, stood by him at all times. From the very inception of the Ramakrishna Order Swamiji felt in the core of his heart that Holy Mother was lovingly watching over its growth and progress. He regarded her as the *Sangha Janani*, the Mother of the Ramakrishna Movement.

When plague broke out in Calcutta in May 1898, he organized relief work with the help of the members of the monastery and lay disciples. After the plague was under control, the Swami and his Western disciples left for Naini Tal and Almora. This was a period of great preparation and training for his Western disciples, especially Sister Nivedita. On 16 June, the Swami left for Kashmir with some of these disciples. This trip to Kashmir was an unforgettable experience both for the Swami and for the disciples. At the end of July, the Swami journeyed with Sister Nivedita to the holy shrine of Amarnath. Observing meticulously every little practice demanded by custom, the Swami reached the cave of Amarnath on 2 August, wearing only a loin-cloth, his body besmeared with ashes. His whole frame was trembling with emotion; a great mystical experience came over him of which he never spoke, beyond saying that Shiva Himself appeared before him. Some time after this pilgrimage, the Swami's devotion concentrated itself in turn on the Divine Mother. Absorbed most of the time in thought of Her, he longed for Her revelation. And one evening it came, and in a fever of inspiration he wrote his famous poem, 'Kali the Mother'. This was followed by a lonely visit to Kshir Bhavani, the shrine of the Mother Goddess, a few miles away from Srinagar. This proved to be another memorable experience for the Swami. He was full of the Mother and said, quoting from his own poem: 'It all came true, every word of it; and I have proved it, for I have hugged the form of Death.'

When he reached Calcutta on 18 October, he was pale and weak and suffering from various ailments. Despite this, he engaged himself in numerous activities. A piece of land had been acquired at Belur on the west bank of the Ganga, five miles above Calcutta, and the construction of the new monastery had started. In January 1899, the monks moved to the new monastery, the now famous Belur Math. The Nivedita Girls' School had been inaugurated earlier. The Bengali monthly *Udbodhan* was also started at this time. And the Seviers fulfilled the Swami's dream of having a monastery in the Himalayas, by starting the Advaita Ashrama at Mayavati, Pithoragarh, in March 1899. The English monthly *Prabuddha Bharata* had been started at Madras earlier, but on the untimely passing away of its editor in 1898, it ceased publication for a month. The monthly was started again at Almora under the editorship of Swami Swarupananda, a disciple of Swami Vivekananda, and in 1899 it was transferred to the Advaita Ashrama at Mayavati.

During this period, the Swami constantly inspired the *sannyasins* and *brahmacharins* at the Math towards a life of intense spirituality and service, for one's own emancipation and the good of one's fellow men—*Atmano mokshartham jagaddhitaya cha*, as he put it.

But the Swami's health was failing. And his plan to revisit the West was welcomed by his brother monks in the hope that this would improve his health.

'Political greatness or military power is never the mission of our race; it never was, and mark my words, it never will be. But there has been the other mission given to us, which is to conserve, to preserve, to accumulate, as it were, into a dynamo, all the spiritual energy of the race, and that concentrated energy is to pour forth in a deluge on the world, whenever circumstances are propitious.'

From 'First Public Lecture in the East'

In Colombo, January 1897
(both pictures)

'Thus, in the past, we read in history, that whenever there arose a great conquering nation uniting the different races of the world, binding India with the other races, taking her out, as it were, from her loneliness, and from her aloofness from the rest of the world, into which she again and again cast herself, that whenever such function has been brought about, the result has been the flooding of the world with Indian spiritual ideas. ... Those who keep their eyes open, those who understand the workings in the mind of the different nations of the West, those who are thinkers and study the different nations, will find the immense change that has been produced in the tone, the procedure, in the methods, and in the literature of the world by this slow, never-ceasing permeation of Indian thought.'

From 'First Public Lecture in the East'

In Colombo, January 1897

'If there is any crying sin in India at this time it is this slavery. Everyone wants to command, and no one wants to obey; and this is owing to the absence of that wonderful Brahmacharya system of yore. First, learn to obey. The command will come by itself. Always first learn to be a servant, and then you will be fit to be a master. Avoid this jealousy, and you will do great works that have yet to be done.'

Ramnad: the house in which Vivekananda stayed in 1897

The firing of cannon announced to the waiting thousands the arrival of the Swami. Marks of rejoicing and festivity were everywhere in evidence. The Swami was driven in the State carriage; accompanied by the Raja's own bodyguard under the command of his brother, while the Raja himself directed the course of the procession on foot. Both Indian and European music added life to the already lively proceedings, the latter playing 'See the Conquering Hero Comes.'

Balaram Bose's house in Calcutta

On 1 May 1897 Swami Vivekananda called a meeting at Balaram Bose's house to establish the Ramakrishna Mission. He said on the occasion: 'This Association will bear the name of him in whose name we have become sannyasins, taking whom as your ideal you are leading the life of householders in the field of activity of this samsara, and whose holy name and the influence of whose unique life and teachings have, within twelve years of his passing away, spread in such an unthought-of way both in the East and the West. Let this sangha, or organization, be therefore named the Ramakrishna Mission. We are only the servants of the Master. May you all help us in this work.'

At Bosepara Lane, Calcutta 1897

Left to right: Swamis Trigunatitananda, Shivananda, Vivekananda, Turiyananda and Brahmananda
Sitting on floor: Swami Sadananda

In a houseboat in Kashmir, 1898 (Left to right): Miss MacLeod, Swami Vivekananda, Mrs. Ole Bull, Sister Nivedita

'Amongst his own, the ignorant loved him as much as scholars and statesmen. The boatman watched the river in his absence, for his return, and servants disputed with guests to do him service. And through it all, the veil of playfulness was never dropped. "They played with the Lord," and instinctively they knew it. To those who have known such hours, life is richer and sweeter.'

Sister Nivedita

In Kashmir (Left to right): Miss MacLeod, Mrs. Ole Bull Swami Vivekananda Sister Nivedita

In Kashmir, 1897
Sitting on chairs (left to right): Swamis Sadananda, Vivekananda, Niranjanananda, and Dhirananda.

'A man came one day to ask a question, and the Swami, in monastic dress and with shaven head, happened to enter. "Ought one to seek an opportunity of death in defence of right, or ... learn never to react?" was the problem put to him. "I am for no reaction", said the Swami, speaking slowly and with a long pause. Then he added, "— for *sannyasins*. Self-defence for the householder!"'

SISTER NIVEDITA

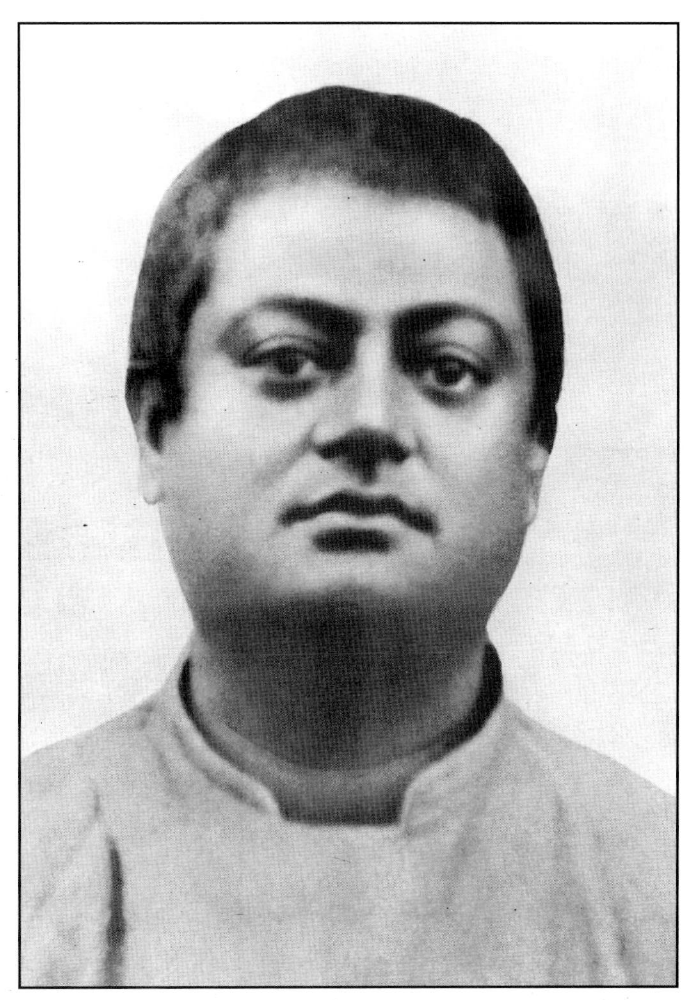

Closeup of Swamiji from the above picture

On the way to Amarnath

The Swami had observed every rite of the pilgrimage, as he came along. He had told his beads, kept fasts, and bathed in the ice-cold waters of five streams in succession, crossing the river-gravels on our second day. And now, as he entered the cave, it seemed to him as if he saw Shiva made visible before him.

Ice-linga, Amarnath Cave

The Swami's body was covered with ashes, his face aflame with supreme devotion to Shiva. He entered the shrine itself, nude except for a loin-cloth; and kneeling in adoration he bowed low before the Lord. A song of praise from a hundred throats resounded in the cave, and the shining purity of the great ice-linga overpowered him. He almost swooned with emotion. A great mystical experience came over him.

Kali the mother

The stars are blotted out,
The clouds are covering clouds,
It is darkness vibrant sonant;
~~In the~~ In the roaring whirling wind,
are the souls of a million lunatics;
Just loosed from prison house,
wrenching trees by the roots,
Sweeping all from the path.
The sea has joined the fray,
and swirls up mountain-waves.
to reach the pitchy sky.
The flash of lurid light
reveals on every side
a thousand thousand shades
of death begrimmed and black;
Scattering plagues and sorrows,
Dancing mad with joy.
Come mother Come.

For terror is thy name,
Death is in thy breath,
And every shaking step,
destroys a world for e'er.
time = Kali (f) Thou "time" the all destroyer.
~~Then~~ Come O mother Come

Who dares misery love,
and hug the ~~form~~ of death,
Enjoy destructions dance,
To him the mother comes.

Facsimile of Swami Vivekananda's handwriting

Kshir Bhavani Temple, Kashmir, as it was then

One day, in Kashmir, the Swami ha been pondering over the ruins and t desecration of the Kshir Bhavani temp wrought by the vandalism of t Mohammedan invaders. Distressed heart he thought, 'How could t people have permitted such sacrile without offering strenuous resistanc If I were here then, I would never ha allowed such things. I would have la down my life to protect the Mother.' was then that he heard the Moth speaking: 'What even if unbeliever should enter My temples and defile M images! What is that to you? Do y protect me or do I protect you Vivekananda said afterwards, 'All m patriotism is gone. Everything is gon Now it is only "Mother! Mother!" I a only a little child.'

Speaking to the junior *sannyasins* at Belur Math on 19 June 1899, Swami Vivekananda said:

'You must try to combine in your life immense idealism with immense practicality. You must be prepared to go into deep meditation now, and the next moment you must be ready to go and cultivate these fields (pointing to the meadows of the Math).'

Group photo taken at Belur Math, 1899

Across the World Again

SWAMI VIVEKANANDA left India on 20 June 1899, taking with him Swami Turiyananda and Sister Nivedita. The journey with the Swami was a great education for both. Sister Nivedita wrote: 'From the beginning to the end a vivid flow of stories went on. One never knew what moment would bring the flash of intuition and the ringing utterance of some fresh truth.' After touching Madras, Colombo, Aden, and Marseilles *en route,* the ship arrived at London on 31 July. The trip was beneficial to the Swami's health.

After spending two weeks in London, he sailed for New York. Arriving there, he went with Mr. and Mrs. Leggett to their beautiful country home called Ridgely Manor on the River Hudson. The Swami stayed at this country retreat until 5 November and then went to the west coast.

The Swami travelled and lectured extensively in the west coast till next June. He compensated, as it were, for his omission of the west coast during his earlier visit. His work during this period was of a tremendous magnitude and significance. Some of the now famous lectures, such as 'Work and Its Secret', 'Christ the Messenger', 'The Powers of the Mind', etc. were delivered during this period. Great enthusiasm was created in the cities of Los Angeles, San Francisco, Pasadena, Alameda and Oakland. The Swami's health had improved after the sea-voyage, and he poured out his soul in giving once again his great message to the American people.

Now the conviction that the East and the West ought to be mutually helpful and must co-operate with each other grew stronger upon him. The mere material brilliance of the West could not dazzle him, nor could the emphasis on spirituality in India hide her social and economic drawbacks. He said to Nivedita: 'Social life in the West is like a peal of laughter: but underneath it is a wail. It ends in a sob. ... Here in India it is sad and gloomy on the surface, but underneath are carelessness and merriment.' The West had tried to conquer external nature, and the East had tried to conquer internal nature. Now East and West must work hand in hand for the good of each other, without destroying the special characteristics of each. The West has much to learn from the East, and the East has much to learn from the West. In fact, the future has to be shaped by a proper fusion of the two ideals. Then there will be neither East nor West, but one humanity.

The landmark of this period was the starting of the Shanti Ashrama in Northern California, which he placed under the charge of Swami Turiyananda. A Vedanta centre at San Francisco was also inaugurated. In spite of tremendous activity, the Swami was becoming more and more indrawn and aware of the approaching end. On 18 April 1900, he wrote to Miss MacLeod: 'My boat is nearing the calm harbour from which it is never more to be driven out.'

On 1 August 1900, he arrived in Paris to participate in the Congress of the History of Religions, held there on the occasion of the Universal Exposition. With some friends, he left Paris in October and visited Hungary, Rumania, Serbia, and Bulgaria, before arriving at Constantinople. Then they proceeded to Athens and Cairo. In Cairo, the Swami suddenly became restless to return to India. He took the first available boat and hurried back to India and reached Belur Math on 9 December 1900, without any previous intimation. It was a pleasant surprise to his brother monks and disciples, who greatly rejoiced at his return.

Ridgely Manor. It now houses a centre of the Ramakrishna Order.

Writing of the days when Swami Vivekananda stayed at Ridgely Manor, Mr. and Mrs. Leggett's country home, Josephine MacLeod wrote : 'One evening he was so eloquent, about a dozen people listening, his voice becoming so soft and seemingly far away; when the evening was over, we all separated without even saying good night to each other. Such a holy quality pervaded. My sister, Mrs. Leggett, had occasion to go to one of the rooms afterward. There she found one of the guests, an agnostic, weeping. "What do you mean?" my sister asked, and the lady said, "That man has given me eternal life. I never wish to hear him again."'

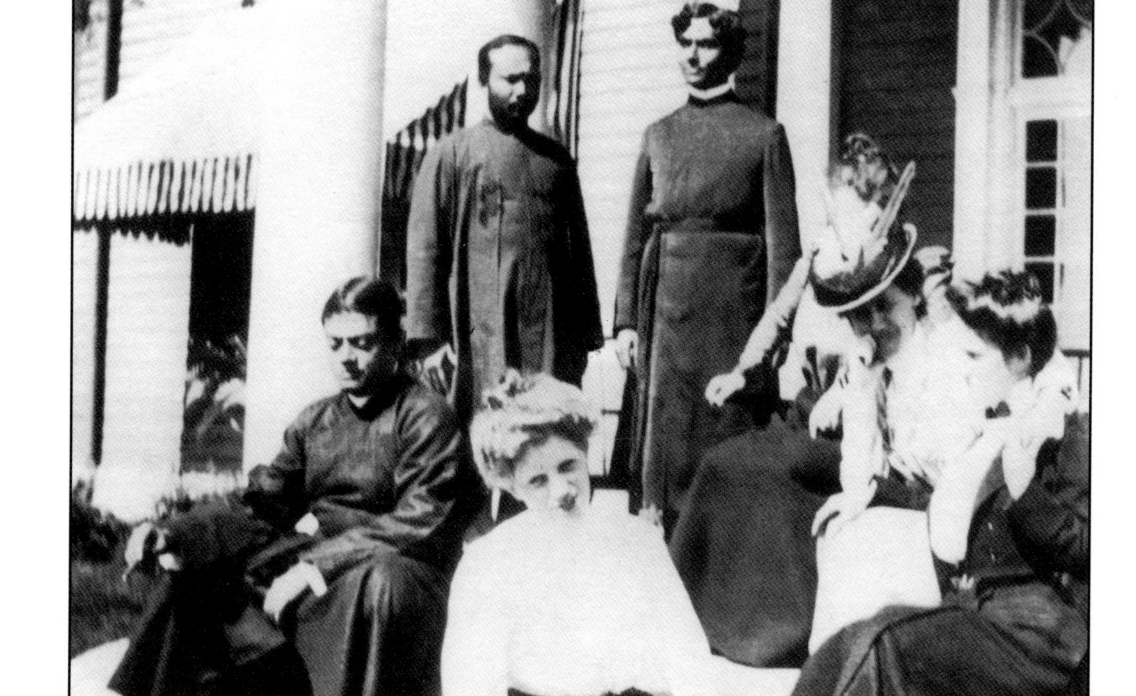

At Ridgely Manor, 1899

Sitting (left to right):
Swami Vivekananda,
Alberta Sturges,
Mrs. Leggett
(partly hidden),
Josephine MacLeod,
An unidentified friend

Standing (left to right):
Swamis Turiyananda
and Abhedananda

'Life is a series of fights and disillusionments. ... The secret of life is not enjoyment, but education through experience.'

FROM A LETTER FROM RIDGELY MANOR,
2 SEPTEMBER 1899

At Ridgely Manor

In California, 1900

'My message in life is to ask the East and West not to quarrel over different ideals, but to show them that the goal is the same in both cases, however opposite it may appear. As we wend our way through this mazy vale of life, let us bid each other Godspeed.'

An early photograph of Advaita Ashrama, Mayavati

An arial view of the Ashrama

'Here it is hoped to keep Advaita free from all superstitions and weakening contaminations. Here will be taught and practised nothing but the Doctrine of Unity, pure and simple; and though in entire sympathy with all other systems, this Ashrama is dedicated to Advaita and Advaita alone.'

Some disciples of Swami Vivekananda at Mayavati

Top row (left to right):
Swamis Prakashananda, Swarupananda, and Sacchidananda

Bottom row (left to right):
Mrs. Sevier,
Swami Nirbhayananda,
Virajananda,
Vimalananda, and
Brahmachari Amritananda

In Calcutta, 1901

'In the modern age it is Vivekananda who preached a great message in India: it is not bound up with any ceremony. To all his countrymen he declared, "The power of Brahman lies in every one of you; the Deity in the poor wants your service." This call has fully roused the hearts of the youth and so the message has found its fulfilment in the service of the country in various ways and through wonderful self-sacrifice. His message imparted energy to man the moment it gave him dignity.'

RABINDRANATH TAGORE

Durgacharan Nag (Nag Mahashaya)
A householder disciple of Sri Ramakrishna

Swami Vivekananda visited the house of Nag Mahashaya during his tour of East Bengal in 1901. But the saint had passed away by then. About Nag Mahashaya, his ever-memorable words were: 'I have travelled far in different parts of the globe, but nowhere could I meet a great soul like Nag Mahashay.'

'As I grow older,' he had said to Nivedita, 'I find that I look more and more for greatness in *little* things ... Anyone will be great in a great position. Even the coward will grow brave in the glare of the footlights. The world looks on! More and more the true greatness seems to me that of the worm doing its duty silently, steadily, from moment to moment and hour to hour.'

In Shillong, 1901
(both pictures)

'He is with me, the Beloved. He was when I was in America, in England, when I was roaming about unknown from place to place in India. ... I feel my task is done—at most three or four years more of life are left. ... I must see my machine in strong working order, and then knowing for sure that I have put in a lever for the good of humanity, in India at least, which no power can drive back, I will sleep without caring what will be next; and may I be born again and again, and suffer thousands of miseries so that I may worship the only God that exists, the only God I believe in, the sum total of all souls—and, above all, my God the wicked, my God the miserable, my God the poor of all races, of all species, is the special object of my worship.'

From a letter to Mary Hale,
9 July 1897

'I will go into a thousand hells cheerfully, if I can rouse my countrymen, immersed in tamas, to stand on their own feet and be *men* inspired with the spirit of karma yoga.'

In Shillong, 1901, after an illness

In Shillong, 1901

'Once in Kashmir, after an attack of illness, I had seen him lift a couple of pebbles, saying, "Whenever death approaches me, all weakness vanishes. I have neither fear, nor doubt, nor thought of the external. I simply busy myself making ready to die. I am as hard as *that*"— and the stones struck one another in his hand—"for I *have* touched the Feet of God."'

SISTER NIVEDITA

An early picture of the Math at Belur

'It is my wish to convert this Math into a chief centre of spiritual practices and the culture of knowledge. The power that will have its rise from here will flood the whole world and turn the course of men's lives into different channels; from this place will spring forth ideals which will be the harmony of Knowledge, Devotion, Yoga, and Work; at a nod from the men of this Math, a life-giving impetus will in time be given to the remotest corners of the globe; while all true seekers after spirituality will in course of time assemble here. A thousand thoughts like these are arising in my mind.'

FROM A CONVERSATION

Swami Vivekananda's room at Belur Math, where he entered into mahasamadhi on 4 July 1902

'Verily I am a bird of passage. Gay and busy Paris, grim old Constantinople, sparkling little Athens, and Pyramidal Cairo are left behind, and here I am writing in my room on the Ganga, in the Math. It is so quiet and still! The broad river is dancing in the bright sunshine, only now and then an occasional cargo boat breaking the silence with the splashing of the oars.'

FROM A LETTER TO NIVEDITA,
19 DECEMBER 1900

Swami Vivekananda temple, Belur Math

Three days before his passing away, as he was walking to and fro on the spacious lawn of the monastery in the afternoon with Swami Premananda, Swamiji pointed to a particular spot on the bank of the Ganga, and said to him gravely: 'When I give up the body, cremate it there.' On that very spot stands today this temple in his honour.

Brother-disciples

SRI RAMAKRISHNA had bound his disciples to each other with a bond of love, and he left themin Swami Vivekananda's charge. This bond was so strong that the Swami could never forget his brother-disciples whether he was near or far away. The following conversation with his disciple, Sharatchandra Chakravarty, illustrates how the Swami felt about them:

Swamiji: These children of Sri Ramakrishna whom you see are wonderful *tyagis* (selfless souls). By serving them, your mind will be purified and you will be blessed with the vision of the Atman.

Disciple: But I find it very difficult to understand them. Each one seems to be of a different type.

Swamiji: Sri Ramakrishna was a wonderful gardener. Therefore, he has made a bouquet of different flowers and formed his Order. All different types and ideas have come into it, and many more will come. Sri Ramakrishna used to say: 'Whoever has prayed to God sincerely for even one day, must come here.' Know each of those who are here to be of great spiritual power. Because they remain shrivelled before me, do not think them to be ordinary souls. When they will go out, they will be the cause of the awakening of spirituality in people. Know them to be part of the spiritual body of Sri Ramakrishna, who was the embodiment of infinite religious ideas. I look upon them with that eye. See, for instance, Brahmananda, who is here—even I have not the spirituality which he has. Sri Ramakrishna looked upon him as his mind-born son; and he lived and walked, ate and slept with him. He is the ornament of our Math—our king. Similarly, Premananda, Turiyananda, Trigunatitananda, Akhandananda, Saradananda, Ramakrishnananda, Subodhananda, and others. You may go round the world, but it is doubtful if you will find men of such spirituality and faith in God as they are. They are each a centre of religious power, and in time that power will manifest.

Swami Brahmananda (Rakhal)
21 January 1863 – 10 April 1922

When Swami Vivekananda returned from America, he bowed down to Swami Brahmananda, quoting a saying from the scriptures: 'The son of the guru is to be respected as much as the guru himself.'

Swami Brahmananda returned the act of reverence with another quotation: 'One's elder brother is to be revered as one's father.'

It was Swami Brahmananda who took up from Swamiji the reins of the Ramakrishna Order.

Swami Yogananda (Yogen)
March 1861– 28 March 1899

Swami Yogananda was one of those whom Sri Ramakrishna recognized as 'Ishvarakotis' or 'eternally perfect'—one of those souls who are never in bondage, but now and then come to this world of ours to guide humanity Godwards.

Swami Premananda (Baburam)
10 December 1861 – 30 July 1918

At Baranagore, when the young monks took the formal vows of *sannyasa,* Swamiji gave Baburam the name 'Premananda' as he thought it conformed to the remark of Sri Ramakrishna that Sri Radha, the goddess of divine love, herself was partially incarnated in Baburam.

In later years, Premananda used to say to the new monks at the Math: 'Do I love you? No—for if I really did, I should have bound you to me for ever. Oh, how dearly the Master loved us! We don't have even a hundredth part of that love towards you.'

Swami Niranjanananda (Niranjan)
August 1862 – 9 May 1904

'Niranjan has a militant disposition, but he has great devotion for the Holy Mother, and all his vagaries I can easily put up with. He is now doing the most marvellous work.'

FROM A LETTER TO
SWAMI SHIVANANDA, 1894

Swami Shivananda (Tarak)
16 November 1854 – 20 February 1934

Tarak's purity and prayer, Sri Ramakrishna's advice and encouragement, and the grace of the all-merciful providence did not allow him to fall a victim to the snares of the world. The perfect purity of his pre-monastic married life earned for him his popular name of 'Mahapurusha', which was given him by Swami Vivekananda. He succeeded Swami Brahmananda as the President of the Ramakrishna Order.

Swami Saradananda (Sarat)
23 December 1865 – 19 August 1927

Partly owing to his ill health and partly to the fact that Swamiji wanted to see his work progress as much as possible during his life-time, he was now and then very severe in his dealings with those around him. But Swami Saradananda could freeze anybody's anger. Seeing this trait in him, Swamiji used to say playfully, 'Sarat has the blood of a fish, it will never warm up.'

Swamiji made Swami Saradananda the Secretary of the whole Organization, the post he held till his last day.

Swami Ramakrishnananda (Sashi)
13 July 1863 – 21 August 1911

In 1897, when Swamiji returned to India, some of the citizens of Madras requested him to send one of his brother-disciples to stay in Madras and establish a monastery there. Swamiji said: 'I shall send you one who is more orthodox than your most orthodox men and who is at the same time unique and unsurpassed in his worship and meditation on God.' The very next steamer from Calcutta took to Madras Swami Ramakrishnananda.

Swami Abhedananda (Kali)
2 October 1866 – 8 September 1939

Swami Abhedananda delivered his first public lecture in London on 27 October 1896. It was a great success. At this the joy of Swami Vivekananda knew no bounds. Referring to this happy occasion, Mr. Eric Hammond, an English disciple of Swamiji, wrote: 'The Master (Swami Vivekananda) was more than content to have effaced himself in order that his brother's opportunity should be altogether unhindered. The whole impression had in it a glowing beauty quite indescribable. It was as though the Master thought, "Even if I perish on this plane, my message will be sounded through these dear lips and the world will hear it."'

Swami Adbhutananda (Latu)
Mahasamadhi on 24 April 1920

'Latu is the greatest miracle of Sri Ramakrishna', said Swami Vivekananda, referring to Swami Adbhutananda. 'Our Master was original, and every one of his disciples also is original. Look at Latu. Born and brought up in a poor family, he has attained to a level of spirituality which is the despair of many. We came with education. But Latu had no such opportunity for diversion. Yet simply through one-pointed devotion he has made his life exalted.'

Swami Turiyananda (Hari)
3 January 1863 – 21 July 1921

Swami Vivekananda once said to his American disciples: 'In me you have seen the expression of Kshatriya power. I am going to send to you one who is the embodiment of Brahminical qualities, who represents what a Brahmin or the highest spiritual evolution of man is.' And he sent Swami Turiyananda.

Swami Advaitananda (Gopal)
Mahasamadhi on 28 December 1909

One day Gopal (Senior) expressed a desire to Sri Ramakrishna to distribute some ochre cloths and rudraksha rosaries to monks. To this the Master replied: 'You won't find better monks than these young boys here. You may give your cloths and rosaries to them.' Thereupon Gopal (Senior) placed the ochre cloths and rosaries before the Master, who distributed them among his young disciples. Thus was sown the seed of the future Ramakrishna Order.

Swami Trigunatitananda (Sarada)
30 January 1865 – 10 January 1915

To organize the publication of the periodical which Swamiji named *Udbodhan*, Swami Trigunatitananda had to undergo Herculean labour. Swamiji remarked that such an amount of work and hardship was possible only for a disciple of Sri Ramakrishna, who lived for the good of humanity alone. In 1903, Swami Trigunatitananda left for San Francisco to organize the Vedanta work there. He carried on the work successfully till his life came to a sudden end in 1915.

Swami Subodhananda (Khoka)
8 November 1867 – 2 December 1932

When the monastery was at Alambazar, Swami Vivekananda wanted to encourage the art of public speaking among the monks. The turn of Swami Subodhananda came and he stood up willy-nilly. Then, lo! The earth trembled, buildings shook, and trees fell: it was the earthquake of 1897. The meeting came to an abrupt end. 'Khoka's was a "world-shaking" speech', Swami Vivekananda said, and the others joined in the fun. Swami Subodhananda was called 'Khoka' (a boy) because of his childlike simplicity.

Swami Akhandananda (Gangadhar)
30 September 1864 – 7 February 1937

Referring to Swami Akhandananda, Swamiji said: 'Look what a great karma yogi he is! Without fear, caring neither for life nor death, how he is working with one-pointed devotion for the good of the many, for the happiness of the many!' He spent his life for the betterment of rural life and succeeded Swami Shivananda as the President of the Order.

Swami Vijnanananda (Hariprasanna)
30 October 1868 – 25 April 1938

Swami Vivekananda had a great desire to raise a temple to the Master at Belur Math. Swami Vijnanananda, in consultation with a noted European architect of Calcutta, prepared a design of the proposed temple. Swamiji approved the design. However, the temple could not be built in Swamiji's lifetime. The foundation-stone of this noble edifice was laid in July 1935 by Swami Vijnanananda, as the Vice-President of the Order, and he dedicated the temple during his presidentship, which followed that of Swami Akhandananda.

The Ramakrishna Movement

Swami Vivekananda accomplished his great mission within a bare decade. He took the old Vedantic religion and set it in motion once more, readjusted to modern needs. Describing this aim, he wrote in a letter: 'The abstract Advaita must become living—poetic—in everyday life; out of hopelessly intricate mythology must come concrete moral forms; and out of bewildering Yogi-ism must come the most scientific and practical psychology—and all this must be put in a form so that a child may grasp it. That is my life's work.'

To give concrete shape to the message of Sri Ramakrishna and himself, Swami Vivekananda launched the monastic Order, which was brought into being by the Master himself at Cossipore, during his last illness. Thus the first Ramakrishna Math was formed. Parallel and integrated with it, though legally distinct from it, the Ramakrishna Mission was developed, through which the Order could carry on certain forms of its service in co-operation with lay workers and devotees. The motto Swamiji placed before members—and, indeed, before the whole movement—was: *'Atmano mokshartham jagad-hitaya cha*—for one's own liberation and for the good of the world.'

The Math was to be the centre of spiritual teaching, guiding and inspiring earnest seekers and moulding the life of its monastic members. It was first formed at Baranagore, in an old dilapidated building, immediately after Sri Ramakrishna's *mahasamadhi* in 1886. The Math later shifted to Alambazar, another suburb of Calcutta, and finally on 9 December 1898, to its present site at Belur. The Math at Baranagore, which mainly comprised Sri Ramakrishna's young disciples, attracted other young men in the course of time. By the time it moved to Belur in 1898, it had become a monastic community leading an organized life.

Meanwhile, when Swami Vivekananda returned from the West, he promised his Madras disciples that he would send them one of his brother-disciples who would be more orthodox than their most orthodox men. This brother-disciple turned out to be Swami Ramakrishnananda, who organized the monastery at Madras, which later developed into one of the chief centres of the Order. He also set in motion the Mission's work in South India.

The growing monastic community needed rules too. The Swami, during his last days, dictated these rules to Swami Shuddhananda, one of his prominent disciples. Before dictating the rules Swamiji remarked: 'Look here, we are going to make rules, no doubt; but we must remember the main object thereof. Our main object is to transcend all rules

Alambazar Monastery
November 1891 – February 1898

Nilambar Babu's garden house, in 1940
February 1898 – December 1898

and regulations. We have naturally some bad tendencies which are to be changed by observing good rules and regulations; and finally we have to go beyond all these even, just as we remove one thorn by another, and throw both of them away.'

The Math at Belur grew as time went on. It had been the great desire of the Swami that a temple should be constructed for his Master. This was fulfilled thirty-six years later when a magnificent temple in the Math grounds was dedicated to Sri Ramakrishna in 1938. But he had himself already installed the Master's relics in the new monastery. On that occasion he had said: 'The Master once told me, "I will go and live wheresoever it will be your pleasure to take me, carrying me on your shoulders—be it under a tree or in the humblest cottage!" With faith in that gracious promise I myself am now carrying him to the site of the future Math. Know for certain, my boy, that so long as his name inspires his followers with his ideals of purity, holiness, and loving spirit of charity to all men, even so long shall he, the Master, sanctify the place with his hallowed presence.'

While the Math was for the spiritual development of monastics and devotees, the Ramakrishna Mission was to devote itself, in the light of the teaching of Sri Ramakrishna, to service in the fields of education, medical help, emergency relief in calamities, and the like. It was also to spread the message of Vedanta, in which will be found the universal principles underlying all religions.

An early picture of Belur Math (Swamiji's room is on the left)

Nilambar Babu's garden house, as it is today

Sri Ramakrishna temple, Belur Math

The Ramakrishna Mission was formally constituted on 1 May 1897. Its earliest activities were famine relief work in Murshidabad district during 1897, and plague relief in Calcutta in 1899. The Ramakrishna Home of Service was started in 1902 by some enthusiastic young men, inspired by Swamiji's message. The Swami himself wrote an appeal for funds for this institution. Later it became one of the chief centres of medical activity under the Ramakrishna Mission.

Thus it will be clear that the object of the Ramakrishna Math and Mission is service to humanity without distinction. In the Ramakrishna movement all religions are looked upon as paths to the attainment of spiritual illumination, and all people as manifestations of the one universal Spirit. Conversion to any particular viewpoint or path naturally has no place in the work or thought of a movement which seeks to reflect Sri Ramakrishna's realization of the underlying truth and harmony of all paths.

Sri Ramakrishna practised the disciplines prescribed by all the various modes of religious thought, dualistic and non-dualistic, of Hinduism. Subsequently, he followed Islam, and still later had a spiritual vision of Christ. Thus it was that through reason and actual experience he came to his well-known conclusion, 'as many faiths, so many paths.'

During the lifetime of Swami Vivekananda, six centres were founded: two Maths, one at Belur and one at Madras, the Advaita Ashrama at Mayavati, an orphanage at Sargachi in the Murshidabad district of Bengal, and two Vedanta Societies, one in New York and another in San Francisco. At Varanasi, the nucleus of the future Ramakrishna Mission Home of Service was formed; and on the very last day of Swamiji's life on earth, the Ramakrishna Advaita Ashrama at Varanasi was formally inaugurated.

In succeeding years, the Math and Mission made substantial progress in implementing their programmes under Swami Brahmananda until

SOME MONASTIC DISCIPLES OF SWAMI VIVEKANANDA

Swami Shuddhananda *Swami Virajananda* *Swami Swarupananda*

Swami Sadananda *Swami Vimalananda* *Swami Somananda* *Swami Shubhananda*

Swami Prakashananda *Swami Paramananda* *Swami Nischayananda* *Swami Achalananda*

Swami Kalyanananda *Swami Bodhananda* *Swami Atmananda* *Br. Jnan Maharaj*

1922, and under Swami Shivananda from 1922 to 1934.

Sri Sarada Devi, the holy consort of Sri Ramakrishna, was a guiding force in the development of the Ramakrishna Order till her passing away in 1920. Known as the Holy Mother, she was a beacon of spirituality and was venerated by all the disciples of Sri Ramakrishna. Her unassuming life is of deep significance to all spiritual seekers. She herself had many disciples, monastic and lay.

The monastic membership of the Order grew steadily, and Math and Mission centres sprang up in many parts of India. In the West, particularly in the U.S.A., a number of Vedanta Societies were established. Thus the Ramakrishna Math and Mission found recognition and appreciation. In 1926 this led Swami Saradananda, who was then the General Secretary, to point out that the people's attitude to every new organization passes through three stages—opposition, indifference, and acceptance. The Math and Mission, he said, had reached the third stage, and he sounded a warning about the 'relaxation of spirits and energy' that might come with 'security of position.'

'Yea,' he continued, 'the Master and His chosen leader have done wonderful work to help poor India and other more fortunate countries through you! But still greater works remain yet to be accomplished, and the Master and the Swami will do it all in time, even through you, if you keep close to their purity and singleness of purpose, their sacrifice and self-surrender for all that is good, true, and noble, and follow their footsteps with that meek and humble spirit with which you have followed them.'

Throughout the world, thinkers came to recognize the importance of the message of Sri Ramakrishna and Swami Vivekananda. It was acknowledged that this message was particularly suited to the modern world in East and West. Even at the turn of the nineteenth century the celebrated German Indologist, Max Müller, wrote on Sri Ramakrishna and drew the attention of the Occident to his life and teachings. Later, Romain Rolland, the French savant, wrote inspiring biographies of Sri Ramakrishna and Swami Vivekananda. Aldous Huxley's introduction to *The Gospel of Sri Ramakrishna* highlighted the uniqueness of this record for the modern man. Christopher Isherwood's life of Sri Ramakrishna is one more proof of his influence in the West. In India, during the years of national struggle, the nation's leaders derived strength and inspiration from the movement, particularly from the stirring speeches of Swami Vivekananda. In 1936, on the occasion of the birth centenary of Sri Ramakrishna, a Parliament of Religions was held in Calcutta, and this brought together some of the best minds of East and West.

Since 1936, though there has been an increase in the number of centres of the Math and Mission, much greater has been the increase in the volume of work conducted by the centres already established. The constant demand for more and more centres, abroad as well as in India, persists. Owing to its

Belur Math from the Ganga

of the Indian subcontinent and the national upsurge in parts of South-East Asia, some centres in Pakistan and Burma had to be closed down.

In March 2007, in addition to the headquarters at Belur, near Calcutta, the Order had 163 centres, as follows:

In India

Thirty-eight in West Bengal, 14 in Tamil Nadu, 8 in Kerala, 7 in Karnataka, 6 each in Uttar Pradesh and Jharkhand, 5 each in Uttarakhand and Andhra Pradesh, 4 each in Gujarat, Maharashtra, and Bihar, 3 each in Arunachal Pradesh, Assam, and Orissa, 2 each in Chattisgarh, Meghalaya, Madhya Pradesh, and Rajasthan, 1 each in Andaman, Chandigarh, Jammu & Kashmir, New Delhi, and Tripura. Attached to these centres were over 29 sub-centres.

Abroad

Thirteen in the U.S.A., 11 in Bangladesh and one each in Argentina, Australia, Brazil, Canada, Fiji, France, Germany, Japan, Malaysia, Mauritius, Netherlands, Russia, Singapore, Sri Lanka, Switzerland, and the United Kingdom.

These various centres of the Ramakrishna Math and Mission seek to serve mankind on the physical, intellectual, and spiritual levels. In the West the work is mainly concerned with teaching Vedanta in its universal aspects and with guidance in practical spiritual life. In the East the activities include, besides spiritual guidance and religious observances and celebrations, various forms of medical service, educational work, rural uplift, work for women, for the poor, and for backward classes, cultural work, and emergency relief and rehabilitation. Thus there is service of the poor on a wide front.

In 1954, during the birth centenary of the Holy Mother, a Math for women was started on 2 December 1954. Though started under the inspiration and guidance of the Ramakrishna Order, Sri Sarada Math and Ramakrishna Sarada Mission are legally and organizationally independent bodies run by nuns.

In 1963-64, the birth centenary of Swami Vivekananda was celebrated throughout the world. An important feature of the celebrations was the translation of the Swami's works into most of the regional languages of India. Selections from his works were also translated into other languages.

The perennial message of teachers such as Sri Ramakrishna and Swami Vivekananda transcends the barriers of time and place and influences the future of all mankind. This influence cannot be measured in terms of visible work done. What counts is the change it brings in the outlook of men, leading them to dedicate themselves to nobler ideals.

An arial view of the Belur Math

A NOTE ON SOME OF THE PICTURES

WHEREVER it has not been possible to ascertain definitely the time and place of pictures of Swami Vivekananda, they have been assigned to their most probable positions.

As a matter of interest, however, we place on record some alternative views regarding these pictures.

Until now it has been believed that the picture on the left on page 28, 'Vivekananda as a Wandering Monk', was the photograph taken by the Prince of Travancore at Trivandrum. But now it has been ascertained that the photograph taken at Trivandrum is the one reproduced on page 36. The evidence available indicates that only one picture was taken there.

The question now arises, therefore, where were the two 'Parivrajaka' photographs taken? The old print from which the present reproduction has been made bears the imprint of a Bangalore photographer. It is quite probable that these two photographs were taken at Bangalore or Mysore.

The top left-hand photograph on page 35 is described as probably having been taken at Belgaum in October 1892. Another account, however, says that this is the first photograph of Swamiji to have been taken at Madras. There is a story that when the print was shown to him he declared that it looked like the picture of the leader of a gang of dacoits!

The photograph on page 62 is popularly known as 'the meditation pose'. It is believed to have been taken in London during a class on 'Maya and Illusion'. The audience, we are told, was so overwhelmed by the lecture that all were deeply affected and many began shedding tears. Then Swamiji had a vision of Sri Ramakrishna who said to him, 'Naren, it is too much for them.' Swamiji then went into deep meditation and the photograph was taken at that time.

There is another view that this photograph was taken in a studio in London under the arrangements made by Miss Emmeline Souter (vide *Swami Vivekananda in the West: New Discoveries*, by Marie Louise Burke, Vol. IV, 1996 edition, p. 521 and pp. 529-30.) But Swami Prabhananda has given cogent reasons to show that this view is not reliable (vide his article 'Swami Vivekananda in Samadhi—A Photograph', published in *Prabuddha Bharata*, pp. 627-30, October 1999).

There is, however, yet another view which holds that this photograph was taken in New York during a class on Raja-Yoga.

There is also much uncertainty regarding the picture on page 77. Some opine that this is the first photograph to have been taken of Swamiji during his time as a wandering monk. It is thought that it was taken in Rajasthan, though he was unwilling to pose for it. In *The Life of Swami Vivekananda* it is recorded that a photograph was taken at Jaipur. It is, however, difficult to say with any certainty which was the photograph taken on that occasion.

SWAMI VIVEKANANDA
A BRIEF CHRONOLOGICAL TABLE

1863	12 January	Birth in Calcutta
1881	November	First meeting with Sri Ramakrishna
1882	(early part)	Closer contact with Sri Ramakrishna
1884		Passes B.A. Examination
1884		Death of his father
1886	16 August	Sri Ramakrishna's Mahasamadhi
	Later in the year	Baranagore Math established
	Christmas Eve	Informal vow of *sannyasa* at Antpur
1888	(early part)	Pilgrimage to Varanasi
	June-November	Second Pilgrimage to holy places in North India
1888	November to	
1889	December	At Baranagore Math
1890		Sets out as a Parivrajaka
1892	December	At Kanyakumari
1893	31 May	Sails for America
	25 July	Lands at Vancouver
	End of August	Meets Professor John H. Wright of Harvard University, at Annisquam
	11-27 September	At the Parliament of Religions, Chicago
	12 November to	
1894	April	Mid-western lecture tour
	14 April to	
1895	June	Lectures and classes on the East coast
	18 June to	
	7 August	At Thousand Island Park on St. Lawrence river
	17 August	Departure for Europe
	Oct.-November	In London
	6 December	Returns to America
1896	End of April	Second visit to London
	May-July	Lectures in London
	28 May	Meets Max Müller in Oxford
	Aug.-September	On the Continent for six weeks
	Oct.-November	Lectures in London
	30 December	Sails from Naples for India
1897	15 January	Arrives in Colombo
	26 January	Lands at Pamban (India)
	6-15 February	In Madras
	21 February	Arrives in Calcutta
	1 May	The Ramakrishna Mission Association established in Calcutta
	May (later part)	Leaves for North India
1898	January	Returns to Calcutta after visiting Almora and touring Uttar Pradesh, Punjab, and Rajasthan
	May	Leaves for North India again
	2 August	At Amarnath (Kashmir)
	October	At Kshir Bhavani
	18 October	Returns to Calcutta
	9 December	Consecration of Belur Math
1899	19 March	Advaita Ashrama at Mayavati established
	20 June	Leaves again for the West
	31 July	Arrives in London
	26 August	Arrives in New York
	Aug.-November	At Ridgely Manor, N.Y.
	December to	
1900	May	Work in California
	20 July	Leaves for Europe
	Aug.-October	In Paris (Congress of the History of Religions)
	25 October to	
	end of Nov.	Visits Vienna, Constantinople, and Cairo
	9 December	Arrives at Belur Math
1901	January	Visits Mayavati
	March-May	Pilgrimage in East Bengal and Assam
1902	Jan.-Feb.	Visits Bodh Gaya and Varanasi
	March onwards	Remains at Belur Math
	4 July	Mahasamadhi

REFERENCES

The following abbreviations are used to indicate the books referred to, and a and b indicate matter adjacent to top and bottom pictures on a page.

Title	Abbreviation
The Complete Works of Swami Vivekananda (9 Vols.)	CW
The Life of Swami Vivekananda (2 Vols.) by His Eastern & Western Disciples	Life
Reminiscences of Swami Vivekananda	Rem
Swami Vivekananda in America: New Discoveries (6 Vols.) by Marie Louise Burke	ND
Life of Vivekananda and the Universal Gospel by Romain Rolland	RRV
The Master as I Saw Him by Sister Nivedita	MSH

Picture		Reference
13	a	CW, Vol. 2, p. 531
17	b	Life, Vol. 1, pp. 60-61
18		Life, Vol. 2, p. 250
19		Life, Vol. 1, p. 128
20	a	CW, Vol. 6, p. 431
21	a	Life, Vol. 1, p. 134
	b	CW, Vol. 8, p. 411
22	a	Life, Vol. 1, p. 183
24	a	Life, Vol. 1, p. 203
25	b	CW, Vol. 6, p. 204
28		CW, Vol. 4, p. 395
35	b	Life, Vol. 1, p. 312
36	a	Rem, p. 101
37	a	CW, Vol. 6, p. 254
38	a	CW, Vol. 3, pp. 139-40
38	b	CW, Vol. 3, pp. 141-42
39	a	Life, Vol. 1, pp. 375-76
	b	CW, Vol. 5, p. 43
40		CW, Vol. 7, pp. 484-85
43	a	CW, Vol. 5, p. 12
	b	ND, Vol. 1, p. 30
44	b	ND, Vol. 1, p. 28
45	a	Life, Vol. 1, pp. 411-12
46	b	CW, Vol. 5, p. 100
49		CW, Vol. 5, pp. 20-21
50	a	CW, Vol. 1, p. 11
	b	CW, Vol. 1, p. 4
51	a	CW, Vol. 1, p. 24
	b	Life, Vol. 1, pp. 428-29
52	a	CW, Vol. 4, p. 348
53		ND, Vol. 1, p. 81
54	a	CW, Vol. 1, p. 16
	b	CW, Vol. 1, p. 257
55		CW, Vol. 6, pp. 260-61
56	a	CW, Vol. 7, p. 476
	b	CW, Vol. 5, p. 72
57	a	CW, Vol. 7, p. 77
	b	Rem, p. 258
58	a	Inspired Talks, pp. 26-27
59	a	Rem, p. 244
	b	CW, Vol. 8, pp. 496-97
60	a	CW, Vol. 6, pp. 367-68
61	a	CW, Vol. 8, p. 223
62		CW, Vol. 1, pp. 130-31
63	a	Life, Vol. 1, p. 492
	b	CW, Vol. 1, p. 429
64	a	CW, Vol. 2, p. 65
	b	CW, Vol. 2, p. 67
65	a	CW, Vol. 2, p. 87
	b	CW, Vol. 2, p. 301
66	a	CW, Vol. 2, p. 141
	b	CW, Vol. 2, p. 150
67	a	CW, Vol. 6, p. 376
	b	Life, Vol. 2, p. 152
68	a	CW, Vol. 2, p. 278
	b	CW, Vol. 2, p. 350
69	a	CW, Vol. 4, pp. 279-80
70	a	CW, Vol. 8, p. 383
	b	Life, Vol. 2, p. 117
	c	CW, Vol. 7, p. 517
73	a	CW, Vol. 3, p. 108
	b	CW, Vol. 3, p. 109
74	a	CW, Vol. 3, p. 134
75	a	CW, Vol. 3, p. 223
	b	CW, Vol. 3, p. 213
76	b	CW, Vol. 3, p. 315
77		CW, Vol. 6, p. 453
78	a	CW, Vol. 8, pp. 306-307
79		Life, Vol. 2, p. 247
80	a	Life, Vol. 2, p. 326
81	b	MSH, pp. 110-11
82	a	MSH, p. 102
	b	Life, Vol. 2, p. 373
84	a	Life, Vol. 2, p. 382
	b	CW, Vol. 3, p. 447
87		Rem, p. 238
88	a	CW, Vol. 5, p. 150
	b	CW, Vol. 4, p. 77
89	a	CW, Vol. 6, p. 425
	b	CW, Vol. 6, p. 432
90	a	CW, Vol. 4, p. 153
	b	CW, Vol. 6, p. 422
91	a	Rem, p. 374
	b	CW, Vol. 8, p. 103
92	a	CW, Vol. 4, p. 134
	b	CW, Vol. 4, p. 125
93	a	CW, Vol. 4, p. 75
	b	CW, Vol. 6, p. 70
94	a	CW, Vol. 6, p. 49
	b	CW, Vol. 1, pp. 460-61
95	b	ND, Vol. 6, p. 370
98		CW, Vol. 4, p. 256
99	b	Nag Mahashay, p. 1
100	a	RRV, 137
	b	CW, Vol. 5, p. 136
101	a	RRV, 103
	b	MSH, p. 329
102	a	CW, Vol. 7, pp. 157-58
	b	CW, Vol. 6, p. 440
103		Life, Vol. 2, p. 650
107	a	CW, Vol. 7, p. 485